A GOSPEL OF
WILD
FLOWERS

Anthony Foottit

With illustrations by
Pat Albeck

D&C
David and Charles

A DAVID & CHARLES BOOK
Copyright © David & Charles Limited 2006

David & Charles is an F+W Publications Inc. company
4700 East Galbraith Road
Cincinnati, OH 45236

First published in the UK in 2006

Text copyright © Anthony Foottit 2006
Illustrations copyright © Pat Albeck 2006

Anthony Foottit has asserted his right to be identified as author of this work
in accordance with the Copyright, Designs and Patents Act, 1988.

A catalogue record for this book is available from the British Library.

ISBN-13: 978-0-7153-2572-8 hardback
ISBN-10: 0-7153-2572-8 hardback

Printed in China by SNP Leefung
for David & Charles
Brunel House   Newton Abbot   Devon

Commissioning Editor Mic Cady
Editor Ame Verso
Copy Editor Joan Gubbin
Art Editor Mike Moule
Designer Sarah Clark
Production Controller Kelly Smith

Visit our website at www.davidandcharles.co.uk

David & Charles books are available from all good bookshops; alternatively
you can contact our Orderline on 0870 9908222 or write to us at FREEPOST
EX2110, D&C Direct, Newton Abbot, TQ12 4ZZ (no stamp required UK only);
US customers call 800-289-0963 and Canadian customers call 800-840-5220.

Contents

Foreword   4
Introduction   5

Flowers for New Year & Epiphany

Dandelion   8   Woody Nightshade   68
Snowdrop   10   White Bryony   70
Columbine   12   Spindle   72
Tufted Vetch   14   Meadow Cranesbill   74
Gorse   16   Willowherb   76
Ivy   18   Sea Holly   78
Foxglove   20   Thrift   80
Oak   22   Harebell   82
Crab Apple   24   Buttercup   85
                                    Red Campion   86
Flowers for Lent & Easter   Fritillary   88

Sorrel   26   Periwinkle   90
Plantain   28   Water Lily   92
Nettle   30
Violet   32   ## Flowers for Autumn & Harvest
Cow Parsley   34   Bramble   94
Willow   36   Corn Cockle   96
Moschatel   39   Great Bindweed   98
Pasque Flower   40   Spear Thistle   100
Primrose   42   Water Mint   102
Shepherd's Purse   44   Reed   104
Dog Rose   46   Mushroom   106
Horse Chestnut   48   Poppy   108
Solomon's Seal   50
Bluebell   52   ## Flowers for Advent & Christmas
Speedwell   54   Great Mullein   110
                                    Lords and Ladies   112
Flowers for Whitsun & Trinity   Holly   114
Guelder Rose   56   Mistletoe   116
Clover   58   Scots Pine   118
Hop   60
Lady's Smock   62   About the Author
Honeysuckle   64   and Illustrator   120
Ox-eye Daisy   66   Select Index of Quotations 121

Foreword

W ord and image, that which is heard and that which is seen, lie at the heart of the Christian faith: 'In the beginning was the Word . . . and the Word became flesh and lived among us and we have seen his glory.' (John 1). Like Voice and Verse – Milton's 'blest pair of sirens,' text and picture, word and image employ their mixed power to lift hearts and minds to God. As in the finest religious manuscripts of the medieval period, written text and painted picture intertwine to inspire, instruct and delight the eye, so it is with this book. Here the words – profound yet simple meditations on the good news of God – are illuminated by the images of the wild flowers that inspired them.

My own role in the genesis of this project was that of matchmaker. I suggested bringing together the two uniquely talented people whose creative partnership has fashioned this book.

I have known Pat Albeck for nearly 25 years. When we first met, I already admired her work. There can hardly be a home that does not contain something designed by Pat – textiles, ceramics, cards, calendars, and, as devotees of The National Trust shops well know, tea towels innumerable.

Anthony Foottit is also a life-enhancer. I first encountered his gentle wisdom, profound spirituality and 'green' theology when I moved to Norfolk eight years ago. I first heard many of these sermons in Norwich Cathedral or in one of the rural parish churches of the diocese where they perfectly distilled the sacramental character of the Norfolk landscape.

When Tony spoke to me of his project and of his search for an illustrator, I knew instantly who had to be his collaborator and soon contrived that they should meet. As I knew it would be, and as you will see when you turn the pages, it has been a marriage of equals. Word and image, Tony and Pat – they have worked wonderfully well together and through their joint efforts all who see this book will be enriched.

Jeremy Haselock
Precentor and Vice Dean, Norwich Cathedral

Introduction

The world's wild flowers are a precious inheritance. They have a delicacy of colour and shape that richly rewards those with eyes to see them and a heart to love them. Many people find flower hunting and the observation of plants to be good therapy, deeply beneficial to body and soul. Dr JD Thornton wrote in 1812: 'The study of indigenous plants … doubles the pleasure of every walk and journey, and calls forth to healthy exercise the bodily as well as mental powers.' Their vibrancy of life and colour reflects the glory of heaven. 'The meanest flower that glows can give thoughts that do often lie too deep for tears' (Wordsworth). To flower and to flourish is the epitome of existence. It is in the wilderness, the wild places of the earth, that we encounter trees and plants in all their natural beauty, and where our souls are most refreshed. Like a flowering plant itself there are several roots by which to draw nourishment in our search.

Many of our wild flowers are related to the plants mentioned in the Bible. 'Consider,' Jesus said in his Sermon on the Mount, 'the lilies of the field.' The characteristics of plants are a rich source of illustrations of Biblical truth, of gospel events, and the lives of the saints. The Bible begins in the Garden of Eden. The Song of Solomon is a love poem full of garden flowers and fruits. In the Garden of Gethsemane, Jesus encountered the terrifying power of evil, which he finally defeated on the cross. In St John's final vision a river ran through the New Jerusalem, on whose banks grow trees, 'whose leaves are for the healing of the nations' (Rev. 22.2). We use flowers to express our love and sympathy, brighten our homes and lives, express our joys and sorrows and help us to worship God. Flowers in church represent the rest of creation in the worship of the Creator. St Paul's advice is to be 'rooted and grounded in love' (Eph. 3.17).

The monasteries of mediaeval Christendom did much to propagate both knowledge of plants and their actual distribution. Their early service books (called breviaries or hours) are often beautifully illuminated with stylized flowers. Later manuscripts have accurate botanical illustrations. It was through experimenting in the monastic garden at Brno that

Brother Gregor Mendel discovered the basic laws of genetics. Many clergy have been enthusiastic botanists, of whom the pioneer is Gilbert White whose fascinating correspondence was published in 1789 as *The Natural History of Selborne*. The Reverend CA Johns' *Flowers of the Field*, published 1894, ran to 28 editions. Andrew Young, poet and vicar of Stonegate in Sussex, wrote two books of delightful botanical reminiscences – *A Prospect of Flowers* (1945) and *A Retrospect of Flowers* (1950). W Keble Martin's *Concise Flora of Britain* was the triumphant outcome of 60 years of meticulous study and draughtsmanship. After its publication with the encouragement of the Duke of Edinburgh, it was the year's bestseller in 1965. 'Out walking,' Martin wrote, 'I know all the little plants I pass. I know the length and spread of their roots. I know their blossoms and seed, I understand their struggle to grow. They nod to me as I pass by – for you see they are my friends.'

Wild flowers are a vital part of our cultural inheritance. Local culture and flora are closely intertwined. In the days before mass media dulled our senses and imaginations, a great deal of magic and folklore was woven into their names. Trees and flowers were peopled with all manner of fairies and elves, gnomes and sylphs, dryads and hamadryads. Their names often reflect a good deal of sexual innuendo and humour. The Green Man represents the spirit of natural regeneration – a descendant of many ancient gods and goddesses. Mediaeval artists baptised him by carving him on the pillars and bosses of churches and cathedrals, and he has given his name to old inns. The Victorians devised the literary conceit of a language of flowers, whereby a lover could send his beloved a forget-me-not. Plants and flower forms inspire so much art and poetry, design and pastimes – from maypole to yoga.

As we seek nourishment for our souls we must not forget the vital contribution plants make to our very existence. Plants make up 95 per cent of all living things. A human body is 90 per cent recycled vegetable matter. Without plants we could not breathe or live. Plants have extraordinary powers. Some live as parasites on others. Some capture and consume insects. Many have a variety of defences against predators – stings, prickles, nasty smells and mimicry. Many have ingenious methods to spread themselves – propelling their seeds by wind, adhesion or explosion, or climbing with tendrils and creeping by roots. Some 10,000 species of plant are edible, but only 150 are eaten to any extent. Of these, only about

20 species supply 90 per cent of our food. Some of our wild flowers have exotic cousins, which provide us with food and useful ingredients from every continent. Several old wives' tales about the healing properties of wild herbs have been proven by medical science. Eighty per cent of all medicines were once plant-based and 30 per cent still are.

The many species of plant life are an international community. Every plant is a complex chemical factory. Coal, oil and gas are largely concentrated solar energy stored in plant material. Surprisingly, wood is a more endurable and friendlier material for construction than iron and steel. A recent development is a house designed on the same principles as a plant. It relies on sunlight, wind and rainwater to be ecologically self-sufficient.

As their habitats have so largely disappeared, it is good that there are an increasing number of people who mourn the loss of our wild flowers and are determined to conserve the remnants that survive. In the wider world we may realize just in time that the destruction of forests and diminution of biodiversity threatens our very existence. The maintenance of biodiversity is vital for the future of vegetation, without which humankind could not survive. The prevention of disease requires the conservation of resistant genes only to be found in wild species. Although the green revolution has resulted in a vast increase of food to feed the hungry, there is generally more reliance on machinery with fewer people employed in agriculture and there is still the threat of plant disease, of which the Irish potato famine (1845–9) is a vivid reminder. The message of the Rio de Janeiro Earth Summit in 1992 is of profound importance: 'Think globally: act locally.'

Many people are fascinated by plants and flowers, not least our beautiful native flora, while a growing number are interested in spirituality. Our imaginative ancestors glimpsed signs and symbols of their faith in the natural world around them. This book seeks to reopen some windows between the visible and the invisible, and to show that our wild flowers are worth conserving for their spiritual significance, as well as their many other virtues. Although symbols and references to other faiths are included, the Christian Year is used as a framework for this book, as it provides a familiar and logical cycle in concert with the natural seasons.

7

Dandelion

Taraxacum officinale

The power of plants is amazing. 'No man can grasp a sunbeam or commit his offspring to the wind: dandelions can' (Brendan Lehane). Dandelions are flowers for all ages. Children love the golden flowers, and puffing the downy seeds away to tell the time. Adults enjoy dandelion leaves in salads, roasting the roots for coffee and making wine from the flowers. With the down blown away the seed heads look like the bald heads of wise old age. Wise men followed the star to find the child Jesus. By tradition they were from different countries and of different ages. Faith often blossoms in the interaction of people, but withers if they congregate too much in like-minded cliques. People the world over look for a star to guide them and a purpose for their lives.

The wise men were astrologers engaged in the early science of astronomy. The generic name for dandelion *Taraxacum* means stirrer, and the specific name *officinale* indicates its use by the apothecaries. The diuretic property of dandelion is well known, and gave rise to its French name of *piss-en-lit*! If our faith is to be stirred and strengthened it is essential to wrestle with the challenges of science. There is no need for science and faith to be at odds. Science gives technical descriptions, while faith wrestles with ultimate questions. It is better to continue searching than to reach final conclusions. Another name for the dandelion is monk's head because of the shaven appearance of the bare seed-heads. Monks and nuns are the pioneers of faith just as scientists explore the frontiers of knowledge. Civilization requires spiritual insight no less than rational analysis.

Dandelions have many cousins. One is the silvery edelweiss, symbol of high mountains. It is believed the wise men were kings who came across the mountains from the east. One of them brought a gift of gold, another frankincense, and the third myrrh, signifying that this child was destined to be a king himself, to be revered, but nevertheless to suffer and to die. Another dandelion cousin is lettuce, which could well have been one of the bitter herbs eaten with lamb at the Last Supper. The name dandelion is an English form of the French *dent-de-lion*, meaning lion's teeth, which refers to the leaves. The lions did not devour Daniel, the man of faith, when he was thrown into their den. Jesus battled with the devil, which St Peter describes as a 'roaring lion' (1 Peter 5.8). His victory is like the golden flower springing from the lion-jawed leaves.

Snowdrop

Galanthus nivalis

S nowdrops are a first sign – a promise – that spring is on its way. Their pure white flowers and green leaves signal a new beginning. Purification sounds better than detoxification, but they mean the same thing. Spiritual purification is by way of repentance – of being sorry and receiving forgiveness. Hand in hand with the renewal of ourselves is the task of cleansing society, by addressing and countering the poverty, unemployment and degradation, which so often underlies trouble and crime. Spring-cleaning is an important household chore – a time to dispose of clutter and rubbish, although it is challenging to realize that, 'there is no place called Away into which things can finally be thrown' (Claire Foster). As much as possible should be recycled, because we are not only polluting this precious world with our rubbish, but transforming its climate by our carbon emissions. Cleanliness, they say, is next to godliness.

Galanthophiles recognize many varieties of snowdrops including one named after a country clergyman, Henry Harpur-Crewe, Rector of Drayton

Beauchamp in Buckinghamshire. Snowdrops also have the charming name of Candlemas bells, appearing as they do for Candlemas – the Feast of the Presentation of the infant Christ in the temple. Candlemas is also called the Purification of the Blessed Virgin Mary – not that Mary in her virginity needed any purifying, but she and Joseph were following the custom of the time in taking their baby to the temple with an offering of two doves. Purification, like the old English custom of churching, had the good purpose of giving thanks for the miracle of new birth. Two old pensioners, Simeon and Anna, welcomed Mary and Joseph and their baby into the temple. Understanding between the very old and the very young is a great joy. When families are no longer naturally extensive networks, old friends and relations become even more important.

The young do not often realize how much they owe to the old, who maintain the faith and indeed church buildings – beacons of light in a dark world. Christians believe that God created this beautiful world, and that his Son Jesus Christ is the first born of all creation. The snowdrops signal that a fresh start can be made, and that it is possible to purify the evil and dross that stain and smudge so many lives and places. God challenges his people to worship and work together to bring all ages into the way of purity, light and peace.

Columbine

Aquilegia vulgaris

The beautiful columbine has some unusual names including doves-round-the-fountain, which is a good description if you look closely at the flower. The name columbine itself means dove flower. Collared doves have spread throughout Britain in the last 40 years. The boy Jesus would have seen them flying round Nazareth, and admired their soft fawn plumage, their gentle cooing and their swift decisive flight. He would have noticed that unlike eagles and hawks, doves eat seeds and dates.

At the village school Jesus would have learnt how in the beginning 'the spirit of God moved on the face of the waters' (Gen. 1.2), and the Rabbi would have added the customary explanation, like a dove. All the children would know that the bird returning to Noah in his ark with an olive branch was a dove. The Rabbi would also explain that the still small voice that Elijah heard on the mountain was a dove. No doubt Mary told Jesus of the time she and Joseph took him to the temple and made the customary sacrifice of two small doves. Certainly Jesus would know the psalm, 'O for the wings of a dove', and understood prayer is an imaginary flight into the heart of God.

Baptism is an ancient ceremonial act of commitment. The baptism of Jesus is recorded in all four gospels. The Spirit of God descended on him like a dove. All these associations with the dove enrich our understanding of the ministry of Jesus, which begins with his baptism. The dove signifies a new creation. The ministry of Jesus is to be marked by gentleness and humility, and enfolded in prayer.

So columbines remind those who are baptised that they are commissioned to share in God's creative and recreative work, to be gentle and patient, and root their lives in prayer. In prayer they may fly into God's presence and drink at the fountain of his love and life-giving spirit.

Tufted Vetch

Vicia cracca

Vetches have several useful relations including beans, peas and lentils. Pulses, as these leguminous vegetables are called, have been cultivated for centuries. Daniel and his friends eat pulses to keep themselves healthy in King Nebuchadnezzah's palace. Pulses need well-ploughed, rich soil. It is a good old custom to observe Plough Sunday at the beginning of the year, although most farmers and gardeners complete their ploughing and digging in the autumn. Jesus told the story of the barren fig tree that needed digging round and manuring. Ploughs and spades are the very basic tools of civilization.

When Elijah first encountered him, Elisha was ploughing with 12 yoke of oxen. To control so many animals would require great skill and strength. The more we rely on machines, the greater the danger of losing the hard won work-experience of centuries. On Plough Sunday it is good to ask God's blessing on machinery and remember that the earth is the Lord's. Machinery now includes combines, cars, computers and a whole range of electronic wizardry. 'The godhead resides quite as comfortably in the cogs of a bicycle as in the petals of a flower' (Robert Pirsig). But they are all made of earth, as are we ourselves. God said to Adam: 'Dust thou art and unto dust thou shalt return' (Gen. 3.19). However sophisticated our work, it still relies on the raw materials of the earth itself – a fact that is dangerous to forget. Humility is derived from *humus* – the soil. Those who produce raw materials must be properly rewarded. 'When Adam delved and Eve span, who was then a gentleman?' was the revolutionary question of John Ball, the fiery preacher and supporter of Wat Tyler's rebellion.

A beautiful vetch cousin is the pink-flowered rest-harrow, so called because its tough stems and roots can impede the harrow's progress. Whatever our work, there is no excuse for disobeying the fourth commandment. Due time for rest, reflection and recreation is vital – far more important than growing greater profits. Old agricultural wisdom also advised giving the land a rest, too. To leave land fallow enables the worms to restore its vitality. Instead of giving the land a rest we are greedily exploiting its resources, and eroding, polluting and destroying the rich diversity of the earth.

Gorse

Ulex europaeus

'When gorse is out of flower, kissing's out of season' is an old joke because of course gorse can be found flowering throughout the year. Love needs constant expression and confirmation. Kissing is a sacrament of love; so is the marriage ring. The definition of a sacrament is an outward and visible sign with an inward and spiritual meaning. In Christian experience the seven sacraments are not just meaningful but a means of grace. A priest often wears a stole to administer the sacraments. You can imagine the stole having a different use for each of the traditional seven sacraments – a towel for Baptism, a napkin for Communion, a scarf for Confirmation and Ordination, a tie for Marriage, a cloth for Absolution (forgiveness), and a bandage for Unction (healing). You can add a shroud or winding-cloth for Burial, which is a sacrament, in a sense, too.

It is by our actions that we are agents of love, by doing those things, of which the sacraments are signs – washing, feeding, teaching, loving, forgiving, healing and comforting. In a church there are reminders of these same ministries of grace – the font, the altar, the lectern, the pulpit, the steps, the hassocks and the candles. Jesus himself washes, feeds, teaches, serves, loves, forgives and heals us. In his story of the sheep and goats he taught us that we do the same to him. This is a mystery – the one whom we serve, himself serves us.

It was at a marriage that Jesus turned the water into wine. By so doing he hastened the process, for water is transformed by the miracle of natural processes into wine. Whether it is new or golden, marriage needs deepening and refreshing – in bringing up children, in romance and passion, and in 'the mutual society, help and comfort that the one ought to have of the other both in prosperity and adversity' (Book of Common Prayer). A recipe for a good marriage includes prime time for each other, mutual appreciation and consideration, worship together … and plenty of kisses. Christian marriage is for life, but has to be lived from day to day. In the devoted care that John Bailey gave his wife, Iris Murdoch, when Alzheimer's disease slowly took hold of her, he records his appreciation of the advice of Sydney Smith: 'Take short views … never further than lunch or tea!'

Ivy
Hedera helix

limbing ivy can damage
walls and harm old trees
– more by its weight than
by strangulation. But it should not be cut
off a vigorous tree, because ivy and its host can
be good for each other. People of different faiths and
understanding must learn to combine unity and diversity to the glory of God
and the good of all. Two-thirds of the world's population follow one of the
great faiths. What a power for good their combined witness could be.

Ivy is mentioned only once in scripture – in the Apocrypha, where
people carry ivy in a procession in honour of Bacchus, the Roman god of
wine. This is because it was regarded as an antidote to drunkenness. Good
religion is the best antidote to alcohol and substance abuse. All the great
religions proclaim the holiness of God, the vital importance of worship
and prayer, responsibility for creation and the imperative of justice,
peace and love. The calling of the Jews is to be a holy people in a
holy land. Hindus and Buddhists sense the holy interconnectedness
of all creation and the human spirit. Muslims celebrate the
holiness of a special prophet and a disciplined life. Christians
see God's holiness focused in his Son. Jalau'l Din Rumi,
a Muslim saint, wrote that 'the lamps are different
but the light is the same.' People of faith are called
by that light to be hospitable and courteous, to
listen as much as to speak, and to work together
for justice and peace.

Ivy is a shelter and source of food for
wildlife. The flowers provide nectar in
winter for many insects and birds enjoy
its berries. The stems provide cover for
snails. The specific Latin name for ivy
is *helix* – a snail, whose twisting shell
the ivy emulates
in growth.

Andrew Young, parson-poet, wrote: 'The snail does the holy will of God slowly.' Let some ivy grow in a corner of your garden or on a few trees. A conservation area is more interesting than a formal flowerbed, and helps to maintain biodiversity. God expects us to live in harmony with the rest of his creation. Ivy also has an exotic relation – the famous ginseng, used by the Chinese for centuries as a tonic, but in excess it can cause depression. Wise gurus recommend a balanced life. The essence of all good religion is to love God and to love our neighbour as ourselves.

Foxglove

Digitalis purpurea

Foxgloves are our nearest native flower related to African violets, whose Latin name is *Saintpaulia*. Although foxgloves are not in flower for the celebration of the Conversion of St Paul on 25 January, their strong stems often linger into the winter. Foxglove is probably a foreshortening of fairy-glove, and some of its many names associate this beautiful flower with fairies and magic. St Paul himself advised his godson Timothy to 'have nothing to do with godless and silly myths', but he could sing (and it is almost a song) of the magic of love: 'Now abideth faith, hope and charity, but the greatest of these is charity' (1 Cor. 13.13). St Paul's conversion began with a dramatic incident but in fact continued for the rest of his life. In particular he came to understand that the way to salvation (holistic happiness, as people might call it these days) is through faith alone – not through good deeds or actions. It was this profound realization that fired St Augustine, Martin Luther, John Bunyan and John Wesley, and empowered the Reformation, which in turn inspired personal accountability, enquiry and observation.

The Latin name *Digitalis* means thimble. St Paul continued his trade of tentmaking so as not to be a financial burden to the early church. Non-stipendiary ministers help link the church to the workaday world. He wrote many of his letters as a prisoner in Rome, but Jesus, he believed, had set him free, even though he was in an earthly prison. It is the task of his followers to unravel twisted hearts and minds and free those captivated by selfish desires, enslaved by alcohol and drugs and the idols of fashion. In judiciary imprisonment there needs to be a sensible balance between security, retribution and reformation. That great Quaker, Elizabeth Fry, campaigned successfully for a more humane treatment of prisoners.

Many thousands of people owe their lives to the foxglove, which provides the heart stimulant digoxin. Foxgloves also benefit other plants by the goodness they return to the soil. Nettles and leguminous plants do the same. Foxgloves have some other colourful cousins called monkey musks, whose vivid orange flowers seem to be playing in the streams where they grow as if to celebrate the joy of life. As St Paul himself says: 'The God of hope fill you with all joy and peace in believing' (Rom. 15.13).

Oak
Quercus robur

The order of creation in the first account in Genesis is trees and plants, then fish and birds, and finally animals and mankind. Science confirms that plants came first in the evolution of life. Plants provide vital food and convert carbon dioxide into oxygen. A large oak will produce thousands of acorns, each one a concentrated bundle of life, and every acorn is like an egg in its cup. An oak tree is a microcosm – a little world inhabited by some 180 species of insects, birds and animals. Oak trees are often centuries old. The Hebrew name for an oak is derived from one of the names of God, and in biblical times they were sacred trees. All the great religions enjoin what Albert Schweitzer called 'reverence for life'. God's creation is, as the author of Genesis says, 'very good' (Gen.1).

There is infinite variety in the unity of creation but also disunity. God in his great love gives mankind a great deal of freedom – freedom that can be misused. Jeremiah saw the world as a clay pot in the creator's hand, which can easily be destroyed and remodelled if it goes wrong. We know that this beautiful world is being destroyed not by God but our human greed and failure to listen to the Maker's instructions. In the last 50 years we have destroyed nearly half our ancient woodland. An African saying reminds us that 'we have borrowed the earth from our children.'

Part of our responsibility as humans is to express the worship of creation to God. This includes arranging flowers in the sanctuary, but supremely by offering bread and wine – those fundamental products of the earth. Worship is the best antidote to arrogance, to thinking that human beings are all-important. Jesus said that we are of more value than sparrows, but that God our Father also cares about every sparrow. Here and there in the countryside are gospel oaks where the gospel was once read, as the people processed through the fields at Rogationtide. St Paul explained in his letter to the Colossians the important truth that Jesus is co-worker with God in creation. So are we. When God established his covenant with Noah after the flood, it was with 'every living creature, all birds and cattle, and all the wild animals on the earth' (Gen. 9.16). He sealed this agreement with a rainbow, a kaleidoscope of colours in a co-ordinated pattern.

Crab Apple
Malus sylvestris

The wild crab apple is a lovely sight in autumn and spring along the hedgerows and in the woods. So are the many varieties of its domestic cousins in our gardens and orchards. Apples are woven into our folk law, and Avalon – the ancient name for Britain – derives from avall, the Celtic word for an apple. It is important to preserve old orchards and local varieties. It was under an apple tree that Newton discovered gravity. The fruits of the spirit are love, joy, peace, patience, kindness, goodness, trustfulness, gentleness and self-control.
The blackthorn with its lovely white blossom and bitter fruit of sloes is a close relation. So are plums, apricots and peaches.

The tree of life in the Garden of Eden may have been a fig tree; hence the tradition that Adam and Eve used fig leaves to cover their nakedness. But that other tree – the tree of the knowledge of good and evil – could well have been an apple. As the old carol says:

Adam lay bounden, bounden in a bond,
Four thousand winter thought he not too long
And all was for an apple, an apple that he took,
As clerkes finden written in their book. (Traditional)

That was the trouble. Adam and Eve just took the apples instead of being grateful and acting responsibly. They wanted to possess them instead of appreciating them and sharing them. It was no good using a snake as the fall guy. Jesus called himself the Son of Man, and so he is the second Adam (a name which means 'of the earth').

Wassailing is an old West Country custom to drive the devil away from cider orchards. But it takes more than old customs to fight the devil. If you cut an apple in half you will find at its heart a star. Imagine your life as an apple. Peel it, quarter it, and cut into slices. What slice of my day shall I give to God in prayer? What slice of my week shall I give God in worship? What slice of my income shall I give away? I am Adam and Eve – I want to have my apples and eat them, but I must realize that every apple is a gift, as is every hour and every day. Medlars, relations of apples, are eaten when rotten, as if to say that it is only in dying to ourselves, that we become alive to others. Apples are symbols of obedience or self-control. 'To him that overcomes I will give the right to eat from the tree of life, which stands in the garden of God' (Rev. 2.7).

Sorrel

Rumex acetosa

Sorrel is a lovely wild flower of the dock family. The tall graceful pink flowers adorn stems clasped by vivid green leaves. Sorrel means sour and another old name for the plant is sorrow. When the flowers droop or sway, as they often do, they seem to mourn and weep. Sorrel leaves are acidic – the name *Rumex* comes from the Latin word meaning to suck, because Romans sucked the leaves to assuage their thirst. Its specific name is *acetosa* and our ancestors used sorrel instead of lemons or vinegar. You can put some in your salad instead of vinegar, or in your pancakes instead of lemon, although it may be hard to find them as early as Shrove Tuesday. Sorrel may well have been one of the bitter herbs that the Hebrew people ate with the Passover lamb, and thus a vegetable eaten at the Last Supper.

A close cousin is called patience dock from its use as an ingredient of a Passiontide cake. Stress is a modern term for anguish of soul. Among the causes of stress are a sense of failure, overwork, loneliness, conflict, self-pity and confusion of role.

The centipede was happy quite, until a frog for fun
Said:'Pray which leg goes after which?'
This brought her mind to such a pitch,
She lay distracted in a ditch, considering how to run. (Anon)

Symptoms of stress include withdrawal, ill health, addiction and irritability. The best treatment is the acceptance of oneself and one's situation with a programme to move on if only one step at a time. Good antidotes are prayer, humour, friends, a healthy lifestyle and interests. But at a deeper level many are healed by the realization that Jesus ate his bitter herbs and drank his bitter cup to set us free from oppression.

The dock family also includes rhubarb and beet. One of the beets provides us with half of our sugar, and in future will be used to produce biofuel. Sorrel is good for the body, just as sorrow is good for the soul. Lent is a time to fast and resist the dictates of the body, which can so readily eclipse the needs of the soul. It is also an opportunity to remember those whose hunger is not just for one day or even 40 days, but every day.

Plantain

Plantago lanceolata

T he leaves of ribwort plantain are shaped like a sword, and children play soldiers by firing off the flower heads. The sword is a symbol of the good old virtue of chivalry. St George, King Arthur and the knights of old inspire us to champion the weak against the strong and fight for right against wrong. 'The only thing necessary for the triumph of evil is for good men to do nothing' (Edmund Burke).

Coats of arms are symbols of power and achievement, but also badges of chivalry and service. The royal coat of arms was placed in our churches at the time of the Reformation to signal the close relationship between Church and State. The sovereign and those in authority are agents of God to keep us in order and provide security and care. Isaiah even regarded the foreign King Cyrus of Persia as God's anointed – with good reason, because he toppled the Babylonian Empire and restored the exiles to Judah. St Paul was a Roman citizen and appealed to Roman justice. The highways of the Roman Empire enabled the gospel to spread across Western Europe. Although he was writing in the time of the brutal Emperor Nero, Paul still advocated loyalty to the state and payment of taxes. In the gospel, people tried to trap Jesus into taking sides. The Herodian party were pro-Roman, and the Pharisees anti-Roman. Jesus' answer: 'Render unto Caesar the things that are Caesar's and unto God the things that are God's' (Matt. 22.21), sounds like sitting on the fence, but it is a genuine holding together of both loyalties. Does modern democracy really need the adolescent rivalry with its attendant waste of time and resources, which has become part of party politics?

The proper exercise of power must always be under God and therefore with restraint and care. A Bible is given to the sovereign in the coronation with the words: 'Here is wisdom. This is the royal law.' The Holocaust reveals the depths of utter cruelty to which a totalitarian regime can sink. Past and present history shows that oppressive totalitarian states, whether Babylonian, Roman or Nazi, are, in the end, overthrown. The Revelation of St John, written in the time of Roman persecution, calls the state a 'great beast'. King Alfred the Great said: 'Power can never be good except he be good that has it.' A just authority gives subjects a measure of freedom, and loyalty to a civil power must include freedom to criticize. This freedom is one that the consumer and client, as well as the elector and taxpayer, do well to exercise.

Nettle

Urtica dioeca

A country child soon discovers nettles through painful experience and learns to treat them with respect. Children realize all too soon that there is pain and suffering in this world and that tears, as well as smiles, are part of life. Pain is a useful symptom of disease. Without pain we could scarcely experience the opposite sensation of pleasure. There is an Arabic saying: 'All sunshine makes a desert.'

But pain is a mystery. Why innocent people suffer is beyond our understanding. Christians do, however, believe that God himself suffers through his Son. 'Where we are, he's been; where he is, we'll be' (Rowan Williams). Nettles must sometimes be grasped. Georges Bernanos describes in *The Diary of a Country Priest* how the priest's doctor had told him that he had cancer and only months to live. Stunned by the news, the priest went into a little bar where the manageress told him of her troubles, but she seemed so peacefully resigned to them that he recovered his composure and courage to face whatever might happen. Jesus prayed in the garden for his cup of suffering to be removed, but immediately added: 'Not my will but yours be done.' However great the pain, it'll pass, as wise old countrymen observe. The joy of Easter follows the pain of Good Friday. Painful nettles are the host plants for the caterpillars of many beautiful butterflies – peacocks, tortoiseshells and red admirals. Young nettles are delicious when cooked like spinach, and dresses can be woven from nettle-cloth.

It is good to relieve great pain, if possible, but euthanasia taxes our moral fibre. Among the arguments against it are whether it may be right to endure pain to the bitter end, and whether, if there is a pressure not to be a nuisance, it is truly an exercise of personal autonomy. One of the greatest of this world's pains is the anguish of bereavement. Jesus wept at the death of his friend Lazarus. It is good to cry and to seek absolution for guilt, but also to return to familiar routine, to remember and to pray.

Here lies Martin Elginbrodde:
Have mercy on his soul, Lord God,
As I would do if I were God
And you were Martin Elginbrodde. (Anonymous epitaph)

Violet

Viola odorata

On mid-Lent Sunday servants used to be sent home to see their mothers. As they walked home they often picked a posy of wild flowers to give to her, and appropriately they included violets with their exquisite scent. What better way to honour a mother and appreciate her love? Mothering is the most important job in the world. Jesus honoured his mother Mary and even as he hung on the cross he made arrangements for his best friend and his mother to care for each other.

Most fathers agree that it is a mother who makes a home. Traditionally she baked a simnel cake for Mothering Sunday. A good home is an outpost of heaven; meals are properly cooked and enjoyed together round the table rather than fast food and TV dinners.

Every church should be such a home, and the churchyard a garden. The churchyard is not only a place of burial, but also a place of recreation and conservation. In mediaeval times games such as fives were played in churchyards. The Sabbath principle of rest on the seventh day can be applied to space as well as time. A seventh part of a farm or garden, or indeed churchyard, can be set aside for wildlife. Another outpost of heaven is a monastic house with its different rooms – refectory, chapter house, cloisters, dormitories and garden. It would be good if churches, especially if they have a parvise room over the porch or in the tower, provided simple overnight accommodation for pilgrims. Blessed are those who receive others into their home through adoption, fostering or simple hospitality. We are ourselves to be a spiritual house – living stones.

Wild pansies are sometimes called trinity violets. In fact, their Latin name is *Viola tricolor* because they are three-coloured – yellow, white and purple. In the mystery of the Holy Trinity there is a Father and a Son with the Holy Spirit – the feminine spirit of wisdom of the Old Testament. The name pansy comes from the French *pensée,* meaning thought. The wild pansy is called heartsease, because it is a herb of love. The passionflower (*Passiflora caerulea*) belongs to the same family of plants. Missionaries in South America were not slow to see the uncanny signs of the Passion in its striking flowers. The leaf is a spear, the tendril a whip, the ovary a whipping-post, the filaments a crown of thorns, the three styles nails, the stamens hammers and the corona a purple crown. The mysterious glory of God is reflected in the flowers.

Cow Parsley
Anthriscus sylvestris

This best known of all the wild umbellifers fills our roadsides and hedgerows with its lovely frothy flowers as springtime merges into summer. Lady Day is on 25 March, when Archangel Gabriel brought the stupendous news to Mary that she would have a son, who would also be the Son of God. Traditionally Gabriel is portrayed holding another flower, the madonna lily. Madonna lilies are not natives but grow easily in any cottage garden, reminding us with what utter simplicity Mary replied to this astonishing message: 'Let it be to me according to your word' (Luke 1.38). Ordinary life must have continued in the family home in Nazareth, and Mary, like any housewife, must have stitched and sewn. It is good to imagine, as our ancestors did with the help of flowers, something of that everyday life. So cow parsley is also called Our Lady's lace, the harebell is her thimble and thrift her pincushion. The clematis is her bower and the cowslip her keys. The mullein flower is her taper, its leaves her flannel, and marigold her money. The teasel is her brush, and the anemone her nightcap. A rare cornfield weed is lady's looking glass and another is called Our Lady's comb. The hay in the crib included lady's bedstraw. Lungwort with its pink and blue flowers is Mary and Joseph themselves.

Many valuable vegetables and herbs belong to the umbellifer family. Carrots and parsnips are umbellifers. So are two herbs, which Mary must have used because Jesus scorned the Pharisees who taxed them – anise and cumin. Isaiah refers to the careful harvesting required for cumin seed. The herbs parsley, fennel, chervil, coriander and sweet cicely are umbellifers, as is hemlock, the poison which Socrates drank at his execution.

Cow parsley is so called because it was thought to be parsley fit only for cows. Milk for the family in Nazareth would have come from sheep and goats, but sometimes from cows, because Bashan, famous for its fat cattle, is not far from Galilee. Cows would also have supplied leather for sandals and meat for the table. They are sacred in India because they are symbols of bounty. Oxen provided the power for ploughing. We still rely on cows for so much. They deserve good treatment, and their products should be fairly traded. Surely Our Lady paid a fair price for dairy produce?

Willow

Salix caprea

The palm branches that people waved and spread in Jesus' path were flags to welcome a king. Because palms grow fresh and green in oases people used them to celebrate victory. The Latin name for the palm tree is *Phoenix*, the name of the fabulous legendary bird that arose to new life from the ashes of the fire. In St John's vision of heaven the crowds carried palm branches. The palm tree was an important tree – vital for the economy of the Holy Land. It provided dates for food, shade from the sun, fibres to weave into mats, and wood for fires. The Passion of Jesus is set not only in Jerusalem but also in the neighbouring village of Bethany, which means house of dates.

Mediaeval people in Europe didn't have palm trees so they chose willow with its silver buds and golden catkins to celebrate Christ's entry into Jerusalem. The catkins of the sallow, or pussy willow, reflect the beauty of spring sunshine. The specific Latin name of *caprea* refers to goats, because goats are fond of the leaves. The scapegoat was the poor animal, upon which, in the Old Testament, the priest laid the wrongdoing of the people and then drove it into the desert to cleanse them from their sin. Jesus becomes the scapegoat, laden with our sin, and suffering and dying in loneliness to save us. It was on willows that the sad exiles in Babylon hung their harps. In the story portrayed in the famous Chinese willow pattern, a willow seems to weep for the tragic fate of the lovers. Baskets are often made from willow withies. It is far better to go shopping with a basket than bring back your goods in plastic bags. An infusion from willow bark was a good medicine for fever – an old wives' remedy that was proved true, because it was from willow that scientists isolated salicylic acid or aspirin.

Poplars are closely related to willows. The Latin name of the aspen poplar is *Populus tremula*, because its leaves tremble in the slightest breeze. Because of this, mediaeval people thought the cross must have been made of aspen wood – a thought echoed by the old spiritual: 'Were you there when they crucified my Lord?...O, sometimes it causes me to tremble, tremble, tremble.' It was the African, Simon of Cyrene, who helped Jesus carry his cross – reminding us that the victorious suffering of Jesus is for all people everywhere.

Moschatel

Adoxa moschatellina

Moschatel is a scarcely known little wild flower. It is easy to overlook as it grows in shady woodland, and even its flowers are green. It is known in some places as Good Friday flower, because it is in flower at that time of year. Its Latin name, *Adoxa,* means without glory. Most of the world has now heard about the death of Jesus on the cross, but it was a very obscure event at the time. They executed Jesus by the town rubbish dump. There was no glory in it – no publicity. Jesus went to his death without protection, without power, and as St Paul says, 'made himself of no reputation' (Phil.2.7). He suffered pain and cruelty and loneliness. He bore on his shoulders all the iniquity of the world. Jesus, with his power to raise the dead, accepted death himself. He became utterly without glory.

The plant is also called moschatel because it has an unexpected faint scent of musk rose. In the cross and suffering of Jesus there is a strange glory. Jesus gave himself as an offering, which St Paul described as a 'sacrifice whose fragrance is pleasing to God' (Phil. 4.18). He poured out his love for his Father and for the world. His innocent suffering removes our guilt, and heals our loneliness, if we will but accept his sweet forgiveness. It is in his passion and cross that we, with Jesus, face the reality of death and know the truth about him and about ourselves.

But this flower has an even stranger name – town hall clock. This is because, believe it or not, the flower head is square, with a flower face on each side. In fact it has five faces, because there is a flower on top of the clock as well. This little plant is quite unique; there is no other flower like it. It is the only species in its genus, and the only genus in its family in all the world. So it is with the cross of Jesus. 'Once only once and once for all his precious life he gave' (William Bright). The flower could also remind you of a dice but the death of Jesus was no wayward chance – in no way like the soldiers throwing dice for his cloak. The five faces could also stand for the five continents. Jesus died not just for people scurrying past town hall clocks, but country people living within the sound of church clocks, not just for respectable people, but for scoundrels and outcasts, not just for human beings, but for the whole world, not just for others, but for you and me.

Pasque Flower

Pulsatilla vulgaris

The lilies of the field that Jesus pointed to in his Sermon on the Mount were probably anemones. An anemone opens to the morning sun, just as the tomb opened on the first Easter morning. The truth of Easter is the assurance that all is well – that, however awful the circumstance, a joyful outcome is possible. Martin Luther said: 'Our Lord has written the promise of resurrection not in books alone, but in every leaf of springtime.' The lilies spring up in the dry bare earth. 'Solomon in all his glory,' said Jesus, 'was not arrayed like one of these' (Matt. 6.29). The angel asked Mary Magdalene: 'Why do you seek the living among the dead?' (Luke 24.5) Jesus is in the garden, at our meals and meetings, on the road, at work, and especially in our worship and in the bread and wine.

The name anemone means windflower – a flower shaken by the wind. There was a lot of movement at Easter. Mary ran to Peter. Peter and John ran together. Then they all ran back to tell the others. There was a rhythm in the movement – jogging, not jerking, the pulse of life rather the spasm of death. To be risen with Christ requires a rhythm of worship and work, prayer and life, order and freedom. Eternal life does not mean everlasting rest. The symptoms of death are no movement, no heartbeat or breathing, and no reflexes, but Christians belong to a movement, sometimes called The Way.

'Festivals,' said Thomas Traherne, 'are the ornaments of time, the relics of Eden, wherein we antedate the resurrection of the dead.' The pasque flower is the queen of the anemones. The name comes from Passover (*pâques* in French). This beautiful wild flower is rare in Britain, and restricted to only 18 sites. Its Latin name is *Pulsatilla* – again meaning shaken by the wind. The Christian festival of Easter is inextricably linked with the Passover – the Jewish celebration of the escape of the Hebrews from Egypt. The pasque flower is purple – the colour of victory. The purple robe in which the soldiers dressed Jesus and taunted him was a sign of his kingship. The victory of Jesus becomes his followers' through baptism. In the power of the resurrection of Jesus, Christians are sent to enable people to find fresh hope – the deprived, the unemployed, the disabled, the imprisoned, the homeless, the sick in body and mind, and the bereaved. What is sometimes called social responsibility is resurrection in action.

Primrose

Primula vulgaris

E aster rose is an old name for primrose. Primroses are heralds of spring. The pale flowers reflect the first sunshine of the new season and the deeper yellow at the centre reminds us of summer to come. The resurrection of Jesus was discovered at first light. Many good stories and films such as *Chocolat* and *Billy Elliot* are about resurrection.

Primroses are literally common or garden flowers. But look at them carefully; they are full of glory. Never say of anything that it doesn't matter. Everything matters because of Easter. Harry Williams wrote: 'It is in this world that we find God. It is in communion with everything about us that we discover the resurrection and the life, and are made new. But our eyes must be open to perceive it.' If we do perceive it, we shall experience everyday life with a new intensity, and see things in a new light. The humdrum will no longer be boring but happy and bright. To use a bit of philosophical jargon, the now is the brink of the beyond. Advertisers have made so many people think their life is dull. They try and persuade us that some new product or experience will bring pleasure and excitement to our lives. But the only way we can live a fuller life is in Christ and through the power of his resurrection.

Brother Giles asked: 'Who is richer – he who has a little garden and makes it fruitful, or he who possesses the world and derives no profit?' The primrose is a spring flower of woodland paths and roadside banks. Easter is a time when many people go places. Sometimes they seem to be looking for something they never find. Do they look for company and friendship? Do they look for a meaning to life? Visiting is something we do at Easter. Often the visitor brings hope and joy, but no less often the person visited gives hope and joy to the visitor. Jesus appeared to people on the road and to people at work. Mary Magdalene thought he was the gardener. He gave the fishermen breakfast by the lakeside. Gardening and giving people breakfast are works of resurrection.

Lord, help us to visit the unvisited, notice the unnoticed,
celebrate the non-celebrities, empower the powerless, and put
the out-of-touch in touch with Jesus Christ who is their friend.
(Author's prayer)

Shepherd's Purse

Capsella bursa-pastoris

I t's easy to be whimsical about shepherds. But it's a tough job, being out in all weathers, often in rough terrain. There are still places where sheep farming remains a vital part of the economy. Sheep provide meat and milk as well as wool for clothing. There are no less than 27 English names of wild flowers connected with shepherds, of which the best known are shepherd's purse, shepherd's comb and shepherd's needle. Sheep's fescue is a nourishing grass.

The needs of sheep remain much the same since biblical times – protection from fierce animals and disease, good pasture, special help in giving birth and looking after the lambs. A good shepherd knows his sheep. The implements of his trade are a crook, a knapsack with basic resources such as food, a weapon and some first aid kit. The traditional shelter for sheep is a sheepfold. In biblical times the shepherd led his sheep into the fold at night. He counted them on the way in, attended to their needs and then slept across the entrance, so becoming the door of the sheep. Jesus said: 'I am the door of the sheep' (John 10.7). After his resurrection Jesus could pass through a locked door to be with his followers. So can he still. He once described himself as an outsider: 'Behold I stand at the door and knock' (Rev. 3.20). Doorkeepers and sidesmen have an important role in the church. A good welcome is vital. It is only too easy to exclude people from our buildings and from our hearts.

The language used to describe sheep and shepherding is still a good illustration of Christian ministry. The minister is a pastor and the bishop with his crook is the shepherd-in-chief. The people are called a congregation, which means a flock. And the church is a sheepfold. It is better to lead sheep than to drive them. Biblical shepherds were not lone rangers. There were shepherds on the hillsides around Bethlehem, and they came together to the stable. Shepherd's purse is a member of the crucifer family. Among its relations are many kinds of capers, cress and mustard. Jesus used mustard to illustrate how quickly faith and the kingdom of God grow. Often the kingdom grows through mutual counsel and encouragement.

44

45

Dog Rose

Rosa canina

I t is interesting to discover connections between England's patron saint and England's emblem, the rose. The thorns recall the spear with which St George slew the dragon that was threatening to kill all the inhabitants of a village. An offering of a sheep a day was not enough to keep it at bay. The villagers started to draw lots for which of them should be fed to the dragon, and the lot fell on their beautiful princess. In the nick of time the brave Roman soldier George rode into the village. He fought and killed the dragon and so saved the princess. Red rose hips are a reminder of the martyrdom of St George, because this Christian soldier was later imprisoned for his faith and eventually executed by the emperor.

The lovely flowers and scent of the rose recall the beautiful princess. The rose is above all the flower of Our Lady, the Blessed Virgin Mary. Of all flowers the rose has been the greatest inspiration for poetry and art. A rosary is an aid to saying your prayers, so called because to pray with a rosary is like walking round the rose garden. A traditional rosary has 165 beads. If that is too complicated, we can use our five fingers to help us say our prayers. The five parts of prayer are adoration, confession, thanksgiving, supplication for others (remembered by the acronym ACTS), and petition for oneself.

The legend of St George (like so many good stories such as *The Sleeping Beauty*) conveys the truth of the Christian gospel. Jesus has fought and won his battle with evil, sin and death and restored love, joy and beauty to the world. Rosehip syrup has a high content of restorative vitamin C. So many places and people cry out for rejuvenation. We all have different parts to play. The wild rose has five sepals, which are curiously different. There's an old rhyme about this:

We are five brothers at the same time born –
Two of us have beards; by two no beards are worn,
Whilst one, lest he should give his brothers pain,
Has one side bearded and the other plain. (Anon)

The rose carries thorns and its hips are flushed with blood, but it bears its own true loveliness as much as any flower on earth.

46

Horse Chestnut

Aesculus hippocastanum

The spreading chestnut tree on the village green is an archetypal rural scene, although horse chestnuts were only introduced to Britain in the 16th century. Their sticky buds and shiny fruits have delighted young and old through many generations, as have their magnificent flowers, which look like elegant candles. When spring comes early they are in flower for St Mark's Day on 24 April. St Mark's gospel is generally thought to be the earliest. It is full of pithy verses and sayings – shining encapsulations of gospel truth. Children enjoy playing conkers with chestnuts – deciding who has the strongest chestnut and therefore becomes the conqueror. There is, in most people, a competitive streak. Mark records how James and John wanted to sit either side of Jesus in his glory, but Jesus said to them: 'Whoever would be great among you must be your servant' (Matt. 20.27).

Chestnuts have distant cousins including rue, an astringent herb, and the citrus fruits – oranges, lemons and limes. Mark's gospel has a sharp immediacy compared with the others. He raises questions more than provides answers. Unlike the others, which recount the burial and resurrection of Jesus, Mark's gospel ends after the crucifixion with the stark words: 'They were afraid' (Mark 16.8).

Maples and sycamores are also related to chestnuts. Their helicopter seeds are quick to take root:

A screaming jet flying high, television screens.
A rocket soaring into space – man's proud of his machines,
But how do all these things compare with one seed flying free
That settles in the ground, takes root and so becomes a tree? (Anon)

There is a strange story in the Old Testament about Laban, Jacob's father-in-law, who used stakes from a species of chestnut to encourage his goats to breed in different colours. The wonderful variety of autumn tints of maple trees makes the American fall a magical experience. The gospels are many-hued pictures of the life, death and resurrection of Jesus. To hear and act upon the gospel is to be as St Paul says, 'more than conquerors' (Rom. 8.37).

Solomon's Seal

Polygonatum multiflorum

Solomon's seal grows wild only in a few places in Britain, but often graces a shady corner in the garden. One explanation for its name is that the dissected root resembles a document seal, another that it is said to be good for sealing wounds. King Solomon excelled in both the arts and sciences. He is said to have composed some 3,000 proverbs and 1,005 songs, and his knowledge of plants extended 'from the cedar tree that is in Lebanon to the hyssop that springs from the wall' (1 Kings 4.33). Builder of the first temple, successful diplomat and prosperous trader, Solomon is renowned above all for his wisdom – that gift for which he prayed at his coronation and with which he was so amply endowed.

The generic name of *Polygonatum* refers to the plant's many-jointed root system. Solomon's wisdom was rooted in his knowledge of the law. His father David's last words to him were: 'Keep the charge of the Lord thy God, to walk in his ways, to keep his statutes and his commandments and judgements, as it is written in the law of Moses' (1 Kings 2.3). The Ten Commandments still provide the roots without which justice will flounder and society will be destroyed. The time has come to recover the old practice of teaching the commandments by rote. St Paul likened the law to a schoolmaster. 'Better the policeman in the mind than the policeman on the beat,' said Chief Rabbi Jonathan Sachs. Justice at its best is a healing action whereby disputes and scores are settled, due punishment administered and reformation begun.

Law places boundaries on behaviour. On the sixth Sunday of Easter it is still customary in some parishes to beat the bounds – to process round the boundaries, and at the same time ask God's blessing upon the seeds sown in fields and gardens. Hedges and walls and boundaries help to prevent trespass and acquisitiveness – wanting more than we need. 'The law does not change the heart, but it does restrain the heartless' (Martin Luther King). The way to change the heart is through the healing power of forgiveness. These two ways, the way of judgement and the way of mercy, are only perfectly combined in God. Meanwhile the courts and the churches both need the wisdom of Solomon, the healing power of both judgement and forgiveness, in every word and action.

Bluebell

Hyacinthoides non-scripta

There are few more magical experiences than a carpet of bluebells in an ancient wood in springtime. English bluebells are a wonderfully deep shade of blue and they always bow in the same direction as if to some unseen lord. It is an amazing experience to be on an island and witness a haze of bluebells merging with the blue of the sea and the sky. Earth and heaven are united in glory.

There are no special flowers associated with the Ascension of Jesus, but it would be good to call bluebells Ascension bells, because his Ascension unites earth and heaven. The gospels are full of arrivals and departures, much like airports, which is why they are exciting places with their cosmopolitan crowds, modern technology and teamwork. It was not like that for the departure of Jesus into heaven. There were no glamorous buildings – just a hillside; no bustling crowds – just 11 villagers; and no glistening aircraft or uniformed crew – just two men in white. Every church should be an outpost of heaven – a place in which to prepare to depart this life and a place to realize that we belong to a great international family that spans the globe.

The bluebell is a hyacinth. Hyacinth was a youth loved by Apollo, a Greek god and hero, who accidentally killed him with a discus. Jesus is the fulfilment of all the best super-heroes – Odysseus, Aeneas, Arthur and especially David. The Christian story is one of love, but the hero did not die as the result of an accident. There is no need to be 'led away by diverse and strange teachings' (Heb. 13.9). Jesus said: 'God gave his only begotten son, so that all who believe in him should not perish but have everlasting life' (John 3.15).

Speedwell
Veronica chamaedrys

E ach little flower of the speedwell is an intense blue and resembles an eye. Germander speedwell grows on roadsides and banks as if to speed travellers on their way. In fact, 'speed well', like 'God speed', and the country saying, 'keep you a-going', is a good farewell message. The specific name for speedwell is *chamaedrys,* which means ground-oak. It seems to say: Mighty oaks are all very well, but I'm just as worthy of your consideration, don't pass me by! There is another reason for the name speedwell. Botanists, like theologians, sometimes use long words that nobody else has ever heard of. They describe speedwell as fugacious, which means fast falling. The petals are very short lived; they soon drop off and are gone. So it is with us all. We are short lived and need lots of encouragement. Wise counsel is of great value, not necessarily professional counselling, but the listening ear and words of comfort that we can give to one another at times of stress and strain.

The Latin name for speedwell is *Veronica*. When Jesus carried his cross along the way of sorrows, Veronica was the girl in the crowd who offered him her handkerchief. When Jesus handed it back, his face was imprinted on the cloth. Pilgrims sometimes carry what is called a vernicle, named after Veronica, which is a little picture of Christ's face. In fact another old country name for the speedwell flower is God's eye. We can see the face of Jesus in those around us, especially in times of sorrow and pain.

St Peter says: 'The end of all things is at hand' (1 Peter 4.7). That does not mean everything is finishing, although in a sense that is true. Rather it means that fulfilment is within our grasp – heaven is just round the corner. You may not think that is so when you are having a black day. But there is always more to life than meets the eye. Jesus said in his farewell discourse: 'I go to prepare a place for you' (John 14.2). He spoke of many rooms in his Father's house. A better translation of room could be an inn or resting-place on the journey. Life is a journey and it is good to know there is a welcome beyond this one, and in fact plenty of places to stay. So we can quite properly say to one another, speed well, as we continue on our way.

Guelder Rose

Viburnum opulus

G uelder berries are the richest red of all wild berries. The specific name *opulus* is the origin of our word opulent. The guelder rose gets its name from Guelderland – a province of Holland. Although it prefers damp situations, it is one of our native hedgerow shrubs. A hedgerow is a community of living plants and is often centuries old. Its age can be measured by the number of species it contains – roughly one species per hundred years. A church community often has a long history but, one hopes, increases at a rather faster rate!

The guelder rose is a symbol of the Holy Spirit. It has beautiful, dazzlingly white flowers at Whitsun – sometimes called the birthday of the Church – like the white dresses once worn for Whit Sunday and for Confirmation. White signifies the purifying, bracing and life-giving wind of the Holy Spirit. The red berries recall the coming of the Holy Spirit like flames of fire. The precious gift of fire cleanses, burns and empowers. Christian liturgy makes full use of colours. Blue is used for the seasons of Advent and Lent, white or gold for Christmas and Easter, red for Whitsun, and green for the rest of the year. Red is the colour of life-blood itself, but in St John's Revelation the scarlet woman is an image of wickedness and abomination. By contrast in the Book of Proverbs there is a beautiful portrait of a good wife: 'She is not afraid of snow for her household, for all her household are clothed in scarlet' (Prov. 31.21).

Elders and guelders are related. The elder tree (*Sambucus nigra*) gets its name not from being older, but from being a kindler for lighting the fire, although only the sticks are good for burning. The elder tree has an unpleasant smell and untidy appearance, which is why our ancestors thought that Judas hanged himself on an elder tree. This dubious notoriety is also accorded to the beautiful Judas tree (*Cercis siliquastrum*), probably

because of its twisted branches. The foaming white inflorescences of the elder are used to make a delicious and refreshing cordial or champagne. They make gooseberries taste like grapes. Not only charismatics, but all Christians are called to refresh the world – to bring a summer sparkle to wintry people and to effervesce with the spirit of God.

Clover
Trifolium pratense

The doctrine of the Trinity is not some obscure theory of clever theologians. It is a profound insight into the nature of God. St Patrick is said to have used a shamrock leaf to teach the Irish people about the Trinity. Nobody is quite sure which plant shamrock actually is. The name means little clover. All clovers are trifoliate, so it is difficult to decide which one the saint used, but how splendid that he taught the people about the glory and holiness of the eternal Trinity with the aid of the leaf of a little plant. The threefold leaf reflects threeness in the nature of God. We experience God the Father in creation, God the Son in the gospels and in communion, and God the Holy Spirit in inspiring music and art, as well as in friendship and love. Here is a simple Trinitarian creed:

I believe in God the Father, who is the source of all things and has made us stewards of his creation.
I believe in God the Son, who took our nature upon him, and died and rose again for us.
I believe in God the Spirit, who empowers us with his grace and inspires beauty, truth and love.

Mathematics like all sciences gives the enquirer glimpses of perfection, and numbers help us remember things. 1 for God, 2 for God and Man in Christ, 3 for the Trinity, 4 gospels, 5 wounds of Christ, 6 days of creation, 7 sacraments, 8 persons saved on the ark, 9 fruits of the spirit, 10 commandments, 11 faithful disciples and 12 apostles.

Belief in the Trinity catches us up into the great love that exists within the heart of God. It is profoundly moving that whenever we give or receive love, we are, in a tiny way, reflecting the great love that unites the persons of God. It is lucky, they say, to find a four-leaf clover. Believers should talk about blessing rather than luck. Finding a four-leaf clover can open our eyes to the grace of God, which is never earned but always surprising – the more unexpected, the greater the blessing. Trinity is not just a doctrine but also an example for a rounded life. James Woodforde, the 18th century parson-diarist, for example, records with equal enthusiasm his pleasure in a peacock spreading its tail, his hope that the price of wheat would soon fall for the sake of the poor, and his enjoyment of dinners, frolics and cards.

Hop
Humulus lupulus

Hops are graceful but vigorous climbers. They climb to a considerable height, with their tough square stems always twining in a clockwise direction. The strong aroma of their cone-shaped flowers both flavours beer and helps to preserve it. It was one of the duties of churchwardens in former times to brew Whitsun ales not just to celebrate the Holy Spirit, but also to raise money for their church.

Hops are our native vines. The first thing that Noah did when he stepped on to dry ground was to plant a vineyard. He then got drunk with his first wine. A vineyard, like a hop garden, was and is a valuable asset, which was the reason for King Ahab's jealousy of Naboth. Pruning is a vital procedure in viticulture – cutting out the old, and tying in the new branches, in order they should receive maximum air and sunlight to produce fruit. Close partnership and teamwork is a Christian virtue.

Church and community are also best intertwined. A parish church should be at the heart of the neighbourhood and celebrate its life. Often it is the only social organization to remain in the inner cities and the remote countryside. The sanctuary of a church is a sign of God's presence, but the nave and churchyard equate to the inner and outer courts of the temple, where people meet and converse. The nave was once, and should become again, the village hall. The nave was an inn for drinking Whitsun ales, a theatre for mystery plays, a court for lawsuits and a market place. The vestry or porch was often the school. Christians should be innkeepers and offer hospitality to all and sundry.

Cannabis or hemp is a close relative of hops. This plant can be a beneficial medicine and an ingredient of paper and building materials, but it is also a dangerous drug. A church or faith community can likewise be of great service to the locality or become a perverse sect, twisted in on itself, concerned only with self-preservation.

Father of all mankind, make the roof of my house wide enough for all opinions, oil the door of my house so it opens easily to friend and stranger, and set such a table in my house that my whole family may speak kindly and freely about it.
(Hawaiian prayer)

Lady's Smock

Cardamine pratensis

On 31 May the Church recalls the visit Mary made to her cousin Elizabeth. Our ancestors in their imaginative devotion provided a veritable wardrobe of flowers for Our Lady. This flower is her smock, and alchemilla her mantle. Bird's-foot trefoil and a rare orchid are her slippers. Among her accessories, columbine is her bonnet, dodder is her laces, foxgloves her gloves and fuchsia her earrings. A rare pink that grows wild in Britain portrays her maidenhood. Violets are her modesty, forget-me-nots her eyes, lilies-of-the-valley her tears, the kidney vetch her fingers, and maidenhair fern and a rare orchid called lady's tresses her hair. In the cloisters of Lincoln Cathedral, which is dedicated to Our Lady, there is a garden full of her flowers. It is good to dress well but we should not become slaves of fashion.

Lady's smock is a member of the crucifer family, which contains about 3,000 species, and is truly cosmopolitan with representatives in every country. International exchanges and visits are very beneficial for all involved, although nowadays we must be careful not to add to global warming with too much flying. Cuckoo flower is another name for lady's smock, because this plant flowers in spring when the cuckoo is calling. Spring and Easter are a time to enjoy company, to sing and dance, and to renew friendships through mutual visits and conversation. Hospitality is a venerable and splendid virtue. Monastic houses have a fine tradition of welcoming all and sundry. Jesus said: 'Come to me all who labour and are heavy laden and I will give you rest' (Matt. 11.28). He was a guest himself in the house of Zacchaeus, the little man who climbed a tree in order to see Jesus when he came by.

Each of the delicate mauve flowers of lady's smock has four petals in the shape of a cross. Even in her blissful days Mary must have pondered in her heart what might become of her son, about whom there were such strange signs and predictions. Her friendships, conversations and visits must have given her some consolation and encouragement, as they do for human beings the world over in their joys and in their sorrows.

Honeysuckle
Lonicera periclymenum

H oneysuckle is a favourite hedgerow flower with its climbing stems, beautiful flowers and delicious scent. It is stronger than it looks and can wind round the trunk of a young tree, turning it into a spiral. Love and strength can be a good combination not least in education and upbringing. These are vital tasks in which everyone has a part to play, not least grandparents. We know the names of two of Jesus' grandparents from a book that didn't quite make it into the New Testament, the protogospel of James. Anne and Joachim were the parents of Mary. Only one person is actually named as a grandmother in the Bible. She is Lois, Timothy's grandmother. St Paul wrote this to Timothy: 'I am reminded of the sincerity of your faith – a faith, which was alive in Lois your grandmother and Eunice your mother before you' (2 Tim. 1.5).

Being one removed from direct responsibility enables grandparents to be good friends with their grandchildren in a different way from their parents. Grandchildren are a special joy to grandparents, enabling them to re-live their childhood again. Faith is passed from generation to generation. During the communist regime in Russia, the Church was persecuted and virtually destroyed, but grandmothers kept the flame of faith alive. And now, thanks to them, the Church in Russia is flourishing again.

The twinflower (*Linnaea borealis*), a delicate beauty of northern pinewoods, is a cousin of honeysuckle. It is named after Linnaeus, the Swedish botanist, who himself named and classified thousands of plants. The twinflowers represent the vital role of parenting, not least in encouraging spirituality and morality. Here is a simple form of the Commandments, to make them easier to teach and to remember:

Love God	*Watch and pray*
No idols	*Rejoice in the Lord*
No swearing	*Listen and speak well*
Keep Sabbath	*Work, rest and play*
Love neighbour	*Be courteous and kind*
No violence	*Be gentle and patient*
No adultery	*Be faithful and brave*
No stealing	*Be thrifty and fair*
No lies	*Tell the good news*
No envy	*Give generously*

Ox-eye Daisy

Leucanthemum vulgare

The first commandment, humbly to worship God, is the foundation of all spirituality. Our faith begins with the affirmation that this amazing world with its light and darkness, its rich diversity and astonishing beauty, is not just an accident. Worship is the best antidote to pride. The name daisy means day's eye. This lovely flower reflects the light of the sun. The little daisies that grow in the lawn only open to the sun's light but ox-eye daisies remain open at night, which is why they are also called moon daisies. Another daisy, chamomile (*Chamaemelum nobile*), is sometimes planted as a lawn. 'The chamomile doth teach thee patience, which riseth best when trodden most' (Anon play, 1606).

An old name for the ox-eye daisy is marguerite or Margaret, which means pearl. One special Margaret is a saint of Antioch, a town in central Turkey. St Paul went to Antioch on his first missionary journey a couple of centuries before Margaret was born. Margaret was the daughter of a pagan priest and was converted to Christianity by an old nurse who looked after her as a child. She vowed to remain a virgin and when her father ordered her to marry the local Roman prefect, Olybrius, she refused. Olybrius had her arrested and imprisoned. She suffered terrible torture, including, it is said, being swallowed by a dragon – perhaps a vivid picture of some torture from which she emerged triumphant.

Now this lovely planet earth is under threat. It is some 4,600 million years old and it has been likened to a person who is 46 years old. Little is known about the first 42 years of that person's life. At 42, life began. Only last year dinosaurs appeared, and mammals only eight months ago. In the middle of last week, apes evolved into man. Modern man has been around for only four hours. During the last hour he discovered agriculture. The industrial revolution began a minute ago and in the last minute we have been turning the earth into a rubbish tip. We have extinguished 500 species of animals and ransacked the planet for fuel. We are on the brink of destroying our precious home. Everything has a right to exist – not just humans, but animals, insects and plants and of course the earth itself. So we must give the creator praise, repent of our irresponsibility and preserve this pearl of a world.

Woody Nightshade
Solanum dulcamara

The second commandment forbids the worship of idols. Idols are addictive substitutes for God, which in the end poison the soul. Like its infamous cousin deadly nightshade, woody nightshade is very poisonous. One of its other names, with good reason, is bittersweet. With its stars of purple and gold, and vivid red berries, this plant clambers alluringly over the hedgerows. A small dose of nightshade is a useful narcotic, but an overdose is fatal. Many addictive substances, from heroin to tobacco to alcohol, have the same dangerous allure. So do fast cars and computers. It is not possession so much as attachment to things that causes us to stumble.

The nightshade family includes several very useful plants, including tomatoes and potatoes – both natives of the rainforests of South America. The French call potatoes *pommes de terre*, meaning apples of the earth. The potato has to be earthed up to grow. So does faith. 'What you sow does not come to life unless it dies' (1 Cor. 15.36), as St Paul explained. Potatoes are not mentioned in the Bible, but one nightshade cousin, the mandrake, does occur. The tuber of this strange plant looks like a human torso and so from earliest times it has been used in magic to induce fertility. Rachel ate some to help her conceive Joseph, although Genesis is careful to say that it was God who remembered her. A pharmacopoeia includes many ingredients from this fascinating family of plants.

The generic name *Solanum* comes from the same root as solace. Religious faith at its best is a source of solace and joy, although it should never be a spiritual narcotic – an opium for the people, as Marx called it. In bad religion, however, learning becomes dogma, worship becomes ritual and obedience idolatry. Religion explains the origin and purpose of life, and how to live in good relationship. To use the phraseology of Martin Buber, this relationship is to oneself (I-me), to one's surroundings (I-it), to others (I-them), and most importantly to God (I-Thou). It is sad that so many people seek solace in addictive substances, when they could find real and lasting happiness in the joy of worship, in contemplation of the natural world, and in the companionship of God's people.

White Bryony
Bryonia dioica

The positive antidote to the third commandment not to swear is wholesome speech and conversation. Right or wrong words can so easily enhance or damage relationships. White bryony is one of many handsome plants that are in fact poisonous. It climbs attractively through hedges and scrub, but its creamy flowers turn into poisonous red berries in the autumn. Blasphemy and obscenity are sometimes regarded as of little consequence, but thoughtless and offensive language poisons society. 'A narrow mind has a broad tongue' is an Arab saying. Racist, sexist and ageist speech can easily offend. Archbishop John Sentamu's mother used to tell him: 'God gave you two ears and two eyes but only one mouth: use them in the same proportion.' The power of speech and writing to harm society also includes pornography. What may seem harmless fun can warp the human spirit and lead to appalling physical abuse and violence. 'Keep your tongue from evil and your lips from lying words' (Psalm 34.13).

There is a special gift of the Holy Spirit called glossolalia or speaking with tongues, which some find helpful in prayer, but which, as Paul warned, can easily be misused or manipulated. Sometimes, as at Pentecost, people hear this form of speech each in

their own language. By learning another language, or even two, people can increase the possibility of mutual international understanding. The art of speaking itself is of great value to both speaker and listener, and should be taught in school more than it is. James said: 'Let your Yes be Yes and your No be No' (James 5.12); anything more than this comes from evil. Beware of euphemisms such as detainees for prisoners, mild physical contact for hitting or passing away for death.

Bryony has some mouth-watering cousins – gourds, marrows, cucumbers, melons and pumpkins. In their hunger in the wilderness, the Israelites desperately missed these vegetables that grew so well by the Nile, and complained bitterly to Moses. It is so much easier to criticize than to praise. Everyone needs some encouragement. Christians find much to encourage them in scripture, which in the words of a collect should be 'read, marked, learnt and inwardly digested' (Book of Common Prayer). For Christians there is even more to treasure, because, to use St John's words, 'the word became flesh and dwelt among us' (John 1.14).

Spindle

Euonymus europaeus

The fourth commandment is to keep the Sabbath holy. The spindle tree bears beautiful pink berries that are poisonous, which is why the spindle's Latin name is *Euonymus*. Euonyme was the mother of the Furies, who were personifications of wretchedness in Greek mythology. The spindle tree harbours aphids in the spring but is well worth growing for its berries and hard white wood, which our forbears used for making skewers and spindles. In the days when every unmarried woman was a spinner or spinster, spindles were really important tools. Milling cloth and manufacturing clothes is still hard work – an industry carried on in factories, sometimes called sweatshops with good reason. Clothes shoppers should pay enough to ensure that such hard toil is properly rewarded and compensated with sufficient rest. Was it a spinster, whose tombstone was inscribed with this epitaph?

Don't mourn for me now, don't mourn for me never –
I'm going to do nothing for ever and ever. (Anonymous epitaph)

It is a far cry from village spinsters to the doyens of the rag trade, but clothes remain an integral part of human life. The French call the spindle tree *bonnet-de-prêtre*, because every berry is a miniature biretta or priest's hat. In France there is a saying: *Aussi fainéant qu'un curé* (as lazy as a parson) but any priest worth their stipend works very hard – often too hard. All workers need to keep the fourth commandment and to take proper rest. The crown of the creation is not humanity on the sixth day but the Sabbath on the seventh. Sunday work and trading is to be resisted, not as a killjoy, but for God's sake, and for the wellbeing of us all. A Sunday rest refreshes the soul. Everyone needs space and time to unwind and recover sanity and health after stress – time just to be.

The buckthorn (*Rhamnus cathartica*) is a relation of spindle, and gets its name from its pairs of shoots, which resemble the antlers of a roebuck. The berries of buckthorn look innocent enough, but are a spectacular purgative. The monks of St Alban's abbey suffered from them, judging by the amount of buckthorn seeds discovered near their latrines. The sea

buckthorn (*Hippophae rhamnoides*) is another close
relation, which adorns the seaside in autumn with its
silvery foliage and orange berries. Its roots and suckers
bind sand dunes together and turn them into fertile soil.
Keeping the Sabbath gives people time for one another
and so binds the neighbourhood into a community.

Meadow Cranesbill
Geranium pratense

The fifth commandment to honour your father and mother is an important strand of the second of the two commandments – to love one another. Courtesy and grace exemplify love. A German name for the beautiful cranesbill is Grace of God. Cranesbills are so called because the seed heads of geraniums are like the beaks of those graceful birds – cranes and storks. Good manners grace civilized living, and have been called the small change of love.

Herb Robert is a smaller and more familiar cousin, which readily seeds itself in cracks and crevices round houses. Its many names reflect its sure place in human affection – angels, billy button, kiss-me-quick, little red robin and jenny wren. Friendly and homely courtesy includes a proper acceptance and inclusion of those of any creed, gender, race, age and special need. 'He is the best Christian whose heart beats with the truest pulse toward heaven, not he who spinneth the finest cobwebs,' wrote Benjamin Whichcote, one of the 17th-century Cambridge Platonists, a peace movement in the English Civil War. Another member of the group, Ralph Cudworth, wrote: 'Let us deal with one another in meekness, calmness and reason, and so represent God.' They exercised a moderating influence in the bitter disputes and religious ferment of the time. Mutual respect is preferable to defending one's own rights.

Flax, another relation of the cranesbills, is now widely grown in Britain and fills the fields with its heavenly blue flowers. Flax is the plant from whose fibres linen is woven, and from whose crushed seeds linseed oil is extracted. Linen is the oldest textile in the world, and was used to wrap the body of Jesus from the cross as well as to wrap the infant Jesus in swaddling clothes. In his Revelation, St John imagines the inhabitants of heaven robed in white linen garments. There is a charming description of a good housewife in Proverbs. Among her many virtuous occupations she seeks wool and flax, and works willingly with her hands. So the cranesbills and flaxes are interwoven with cultured and civilized living, which is so greatly enhanced by kindness and courtesy, and evidently graces heaven itself.

Willowherb

Chamerion angustifolium

T he sixth commandment not to murder prohibits all violence and antisocial behaviour. Its positive antitheses are patience and gentleness. Rosebay willowherb is a symbol of peace after onslaught. It is a fairly recent immigrant from North America, where it is known as fireweed from its habit of springing up after a fire, as it did on London's bombsites in World War II. Pomegranates are related to the willowherbs. Their many-seeded fruits are symbols of love and peace. One of the Beatitudes of Jesus is, 'Blessed are the peacemakers for they shall be called the children of God' (Matt. 5.9).

Scarlet pimpernel is another relation of the willowherbs. Among its wealth of affectionate country names is ladybird. There is a charming French story about a ladybird. There was a murder in a village, and two men accused each other of the crime. The judge found it hard to decide which of the two was lying, because there were no witnesses. The doors of the crowded courthouse were open because it was a hot day. A ladybird flew in and alighted on the cuff of one of the accused. He gently enticed the insect on to his finger and held up his hand so that it flew away. It flew to the other prisoner who immediately crushed it between his finger and thumb. The judge pronounced the gentle man innocent, and the one who crushed the ladybird to be the murderer.

Another close relation is purple loosestrife. St Paul in his letter to the Romans struggled with the divisive issue of vegetarianism. His advice is for meat-eaters to stop eating meat so as not to offend their vegetarian companions. 'No one,' as Paul says, 'lives to himself, any more than anyone dies to himself' (Rom. 14.7). Instead of prejudice, rivalry and jealousy we are bidden to cultivate peace, forgiveness and hospitality.

Almighty God, as your Son was born of a Hebrew mother, but rejoiced in the faith of a Syrian woman and of a Roman soldier, welcomed the Greeks who sought him, and suffered a man from Africa to carry his cross; so teach us to regard the members of all races as fellow heirs of the kingdom of Jesus Christ our Lord. Amen. (Anonymous prayer)

77

Sea Holly

Eryngium maritimum

The positive challenge of the seventh commandment not to commit adultery is faithfulness in marriage. Sea holly might seem a strange plant to illustrate loyalty. It is a noble plant of luxurious greyness with flowers of metallic blue. It thrives on sand dunes and is painful to bare-footed bathers, but its spiny leaves suggest a rugged courage as if to defend the shore against invaders. And yet its roots, which go down as much as five or six feet into the subsoil, can be candied and made into sweetmeats called eryngos.

Acanthus is a cousin of sea holly. Acanthus leaves inspired architectural decoration, especially the capitals of columns. Marriage must be supported by strong and beautiful columns of love, and needs careful preparation, especially in learning that a commitment is a commitment.

For better for worse,
For richer for poorer,
In sickness and in health,
To love and to cherish,
Till death do us part. (Book of Common Prayer)

In hard times George Selwyn, the first bishop of New Zealand, used to say: 'In we are: on we must.' The acceptance of difference can transform relationships. When a son buys his first car, his mother may exclaim, 'What a beautiful car!' whereas his father may ask, 'Have you read the manual?' A good marriage requires grace and law, feelings as well as guidelines. The family is a fundamental building block of society. This is not to say that other forms of human relationship are necessarily inferior. Religious communities have made an outstanding contribution to society and civilization. But such communities depend like marriage on vows, not least the vow of celibacy.

Most churches now recognize the tragedy of failed marriages and make provision for divorcees to remarry, provided certain conditions are fulfilled, including an assurance that the proposed second marriage did not lead to the break-up of the first. Like the prickly leaves of sea holly for unwary bathers, such procedures can be painful for all concerned, and are to be avoided if possible. Nonetheless, those who are involved need prayer and practical help to ensure especially that any children, who are particularly vulnerable, are hurt as little as possible. The churches can provide a wider family for those whose experience of human relationships is unfulfilled or scarred.

Thrift

Armeria maritima

The eighth commandment not to steal is illustrated by this delightful little plant of the seaside, where its velvet cushions often carpet the dunes and cliffs. The word thrift is derived from thrive and originally described a flourishing state, but its meaning devolved to flourishing under meagre conditions with few resources. This plant thrives in rocky crevices and on precarious outcrops. It was portrayed on old threepenny bits as an encouragement to people to save. Once upon a time thrift was a much-admired virtue until superseded by the admonition to increase and grow above all other considerations.

At least half the world's troubles are caused by varieties of theft – of taking more than one's fair share of this world's goods – of profits or resources, so that others are deprived and marginalized. The peoples of the first and second worlds guzzle resources and thereby deprive the third world, as well as threaten the stability of planet earth. We need to relearn the old virtue of thrift and how to manage with less. We need to concentrate on limitation rather than constant growth. A limited, simple life can be very beautiful, as witnessed by those who take a vow of poverty to live the religious life in monastic communities. Should there be a maximum as well as a minimum wage? Should we not pay fair prices for goods or services rather than buying from those who profit by knocking down the due rewards

of producers and workers? Should we not stop using euphemisms and call such profiteering stealing and theft?

Thrift has another delightful name – Our Lady's pincushion. The domestic life of the Holy Family in Nazareth was probably frugal. Mothers used to teach their children to make-do and mend – advice it would be well to recover before it is too late. The resources of this world are finite. There is no blank cheque. It is only too easy to overeat, overcater and overfill. The average vegetable travels 600 miles from field to trolley. Food is best locally grown, organic, animal-friendly, fairly traded (remembered by the acronym LOAF) and seasonal. Using public transport, sharing lifts, switching off lights and machinery not in use, and wearing warmer clothes in winter, are all ways to conserve energy. It is commendable to make an audit of our energy use and, to use Dean Horace Dammers' memorable phrase, 'to live more simply that others may simply live.'

Harebell

Campanula rotundifolia

The ninth commandment forbids false witness, and its counterpart is to tell good news. The delicate flowers of the harebell are silent witnesses to the glory of God. The harebell is the bluebell of Scotland, where it graces so many banks, heaths and hillsides. Some say its name was originally hair-bell, which well describes the slender thread-like stalks on which the bells hang.

Bells are used for announcements. Those with news had best announce it with simplicity and avoid jargon, spin, hype and exaggeration, but certainly not boringly. Bishop Montgomery-Campbell of London, who was trying to listen to a boring speaker, discovered his neighbour had lost his voice. He whispered to him: 'If it is infectious, do go and sit next to the speaker!' Stories, illustrations, humour and brevity are good antidotes to boredom. An interesting speaker uses plenty of variety in pitch, pace and power. In some churches you will find carved or painted a little eavesdropping demon called Tutivillius. He is said to record on a scroll, to be read on the day of judgement, idle gossip and words slurred or misspoken by lazy clerks.

The campanulas, or bellflowers, include a wide variety of wild and cultivated flowers. They are living symbols of the peculiarly English art of campanology or bellringing – using church bells to announce glad or sad tidings or summon people to worship. John Donne wrote: 'Never send to know for whom the bell tolls – it tolls for thee.' Communication now is mostly by television, which people watch too much, so that their eyes are no longer open to the real world.

Churches talk a good deal about mission. So do other organizations with their mission statements, business plans, strategies and PR. It is good to think out and agree what God is calling us to do. In fact without such preplanning we may not be effective. Nevertheless, the best advertisement for God is a pure and truthful life well lived in service to God and neighbour, and strengthened by worship and prayer. Let the silent music of the harebells summon you to worship with your neighbours, for that is still one of the best means of grace in our noisy, fraught and greedy world.

Buttercup

Ranunculus acris

The tenth commandment is not to covet or envy. Buttercups were once thought to be a cure for madness. In fact crazy is an old name for the buttercup. The best antidote to the madness of our consumer-competition-crazy world is to substitute generosity for envy. There is a case for differentials and higher rewards for special responsibility or difficult and dangerous work, but should any human being be paid infinitely more than any other? Someone has worked out that if the present population of the world were reduced to ten but in the same ratio, only two would be European and only one American, and one of these three would possess some 60 per cent of the world's wealth. Fairness is the best antidote to envy. The market should not be a god to be worshipped and obeyed before all other considerations. Trade should also be fair. Blessed are those who insist on fairly traded goods.

Marsh marigolds or kingcups are close relations of buttercups, and symbols of generosity. People don't readily equate generosity with taxation, but taxation is a proper instrument of communal life, whereby each contributes to the good of the whole. It is best assessed on income, but it can properly be used as a means whereby those who cause pollution or damage contribute to the cost. The old principle of tithing, giving one tenth to those in need, got a bad press because it was used in unfair taxation, but it is still a good biblical principle for calculating giving. Strict and thorough accountancy is a prerequisite of good business and citizenship.

Christians are called to be generous. To give up all possessions is too demanding for most people, yet the gospel of Christ does challenge us to make do with less. Mediaeval moralists denounced the sin of usury – lending at interest. The slavery of debt bedevils peaceful coexistence. The jubilee was a good Jewish practice whereby every 50 years all debtors were released and life returned to a level playing field. Better still simply to give. St John asked in his first letter: 'If anyone has this world's goods and sees his brother in need, yet closes his heart against him, how does God's love abide in him?' (1 John 3.17).

Red Campion
Silene dioica

This much-loved flower of woods and hedgerows is a red champion, which is really the same word as campion. So it is a good symbol for a martyr – St Bartholomew, for example, who is celebrated on 24 August. Bartholomew is almost certainly the same man as Nathaniel, an apostle commended by Jesus for his integrity and sincerity. He is said to have taken the gospel to Armenia in the Balkans. By tradition he was flayed alive for his faith, and so is the patron saint of butchers and surgeons.

St Paul tells the Romans that they should be a living sacrifice, and be transformed in spirit rather than conform to current ideologies. The dominant philosophy of Western society is secularism or humanism. It has its roots in the Renaissance and Enlightenment, which inspired the development of modern science. The French philosopher René Descartes said: '*Cogito: ergo sum*', – 'I think: therefore I am', that is to say, I and my perceptions are the only reality. This gave rise to post-modernism by way of existentialism (only I am real). Post-modernism has some good features – a respect for individuality and the rights of people, and an incentive to engender economic growth. But it has three ugly sisters. One is materialism. In the religion of materialism, supermarkets become cathedrals, marketing is more important than production, image than reality, packaging than content, and growth than sustainability. The second sister is pluralism, which is to say – live and let live. You have your faith, and I have mine. Religion becomes a leisure pursuit for those who find it works for them. A plethora of alternative ideologies has ousted an overarching explanation or metanarrative. There are no sacred absolutes, no moral imperatives, and no ultimate deterrents. The third sister is the goddess of competition, which is more highly regarded than co-operation. Rights become more important than responsibilities, and there's no need to worry about those at the bottom of life's pile.

St Bartholomew's witness runs counter to this ideology, which is not as modern as it sounds. He died for his belief in God, which is the only true basis for recognizing the rights of all people and all creatures. He died for his belief that Christ died and rose to rescue humanity from itself. He died as a witness to the absolute imperative of love and care for others. He was indeed a champion of the faith.

86

Fritillary

Fritillaria meleagris

The extraordinary chequer-patterned flowers of this member of the lily family are strikingly beautiful. They flourish in a very few English water meadows. One such place is Magdalen College, Oxford. Fritillaries are probably not indigenous but have escaped from gardens and become established in conditions that suit them. Their cousins, the tulips, were first cultivated in the gardens of the Ottomans and Sultans, from where European horticulturists imported them, notably during the great craze, known as tulipomania, of the 17th century. Tulips are called turbans in Turkey, and may well be the rose of Sharon of the Bible. The fritillary can be for us a symbol of Islam, which forbids the depiction of human and animal forms, but rejoices in geometric patterns and symmetrical designs, which are often drawn from flowers and foliage. Fritillary means a dice box. The religion a person professes is usually a matter of upbringing and therefore, in a sense, of chance.

Christians should seek to understand the religion established by Mohammed, the charismatic prophet who transformed the polytheism of his locality into an all-embracing monotheistic faith, and whose followers number one fifth of the human race. They should be ashamed of the crusades, which are still ingrained in the memory of the Islamic world. The inspired utterances of Mohammed which make up the Koran are revered, recited, chanted and reproduced in exquisite calligraphy, and in which Jesus is named 93 times. Mohammed said: 'There shall be no compulsion in religion', and, at its best, Islam is a tolerant faith. Islam is derived from the same verbal root as shalom, which is Hebrew for peace. Muslims invented the alphabet and mathematics, without which cathedrals could not have been built.

Many people of Islamic faith are now naturalized British citizens, just as fritillaries are now naturalized in English water meadows. Among things Christians can learn from Islam is the absolute holiness of God, a disciplined pattern of prayer five times a day, almsgiving amounting to two-and-a-half per cent of capital annually, fasting and pilgrimage to Mecca. These are the five pillars of Islam, symbolized by the five-pointed star.

Periwinkle

Vinca major

Although often naturalized, periwinkles are immigrant flowers.
Their extended family includes many species in India and the Far
East, so periwinkles help us to focus on Hinduism and religions
that venerate the spirits and forces of the natural world. Not unrelated to
Hinduism are many holistic practices and forms of folk religion, which
people have rediscovered and find helpful. It is not for Christians to
condemn or feel superior to people of other faiths, but rather to appreciate
and learn. The great Christian festivals incorporate customs drawn from
older faiths that preceded them.

In Hinduism all life is interconnected. Many gods and goddesses
represent the power of Brahman, the supreme spirit. There is widespread
belief in reincarnation as stages on the way to enlightenment. Purification
through washing, especially in the sacred waters of the River Ganges, is an
important ritual. The non-violence of Mahatma Gandhi is a shining example
of Hindu spirituality. The reformations of Hinduism include Jainism, which
teaches strict vegetarianism, and Sikhism, which preaches tolerance of other
faiths, not least of Islam.

An infusion of periwinkles was once used to relieve pain. One of
the best relaxing beverages is the most ubiquitous drink after water – tea.
Surprisingly the tea bush itself is a species of camellia. Tea was originally

grown in monastic gardens. Buddhists value drinking it as an aid to enlightenment – the others being walking, sitting silently and feeding fish. Tea is a mild stimulant and John Wesley encouraged tea-drinking to induce religious fervour. The Japanese developed the practice into an elaborate ceremony and even in Victorian England afternoon tea was a social ritual in all classes of society. Often people who claim no religious allegiance practise rituals and liturgies in what is sometimes called implicit religion. The many rituals of sport, drama, music and art often have some underlying spirituality. There is nothing worse than bad religion and it is important to get it right, but sometimes the enquirer may find enlightenment in very unexpected places.

Water Lily

Nymphaea alba

Our beautiful native water lily is a cousin of the sacred blue lotus, which inspired the decoration of the pillars in Solomon's temple (1 Kings 7.22). Water lilies bloom in still waters and reflect the beauty of a god-centred life. Buddhists seek nirvana (which literally means no wind) through progressive spiritual experience (karma). This is by way of the four noble truths – that life involves suffering, that the cause is greed, that this must be recognized, and that it is best overcome by following the eight-fold path. This path means having a right view, right knowledge, right speech, right bearing, right action, right work, right effort and right mind. Prayer should be continuous like a wheel for which a traditional symbol is a circular mandala, like a rose window. Most Westerners find it hard work to adopt the lotus position, but posture is important in prayer. Christians have much to learn about contemplation from their Buddhist friends. Some find it helpful to be aware of their breathing – in for life, out for death. Some enjoy an occasional retreat in a religious house.

The seedpods of the yellow water lily (*Nuphar lutea*) are called brandy bottles, which they do indeed resemble. Prayer can be an intoxication of the soul for which, needless to say, alcohol is no substitute! Frogs love water lilies. The extraordinary transformation of tadpoles into frogs and their ability to leap make them good symbols of prayer. St Benno once passed a frog croaking in a marsh and bade it be silent. After he had gone on a little way, he recalled the verse from the Benedicite, 'O ye whales and all that move in the waters, bless ye the Lord.' The account continues: 'Fearing lest the singing of the frogs might perchance be more agreeable to God than his own praying, he again issued his command that they should praise God in their accustomed fashion: and soon the air and fields were vehement with their conversation.'
(Helen Waddell)

Bramble
Rubus fruticosus

B lackberrying is one of life's simple pleasures. There is the luscious fruit by courtesy of the farmers who don't trim their hedges too soon. But there are disadvantages – your hands get stained with juice, and pricked by the sharp thorns. Blackberries are a marvellous symbol of grace. All for free. Instead of walking down the supermarket aisles plucking processed foods from the shelves, you walk along the hedgerows picking natural food and find no checkout to negotiate as you leave. Blackberry wine is pretty lethal stuff, but in small quantities it warms the cockles of your heart and helps you be merry. Garden raspberries, which are close cousins, delight us in early summer.

Think about the stain. There is disease and evil in the world. Like lots of old wives tales there's some truth in the saying: 'You shouldn't pick blackberries after Allhalloween because the devil has spat on them.' The secretions of fruit flies on the ripe fruit can make you ill. Disease is a mystery, but sin isn't. There's no mystery, for example, about greed. Jotham, a judge in the Old Testament, told a story about the bramble (Judges 9). In those days brambles were used for kindling. In Jotham's

story the trees decided to elect a king. The olive, the fig, and the vine declined. At last the bramble accepted on condition that all the other trees obeyed him, otherwise, the bramble said, he would set fire to them. Jotham used this story to encourage the people to stand up to ruthlessness and greed. The mediaeval Christians preached against usury, which is making money out of money, and in a wider sense means selling goods for too much profit or paying under the odds. Matthew left his profiteering to follow Jesus. Is God calling us to change from an economy of growth to an economy of limitation? This includes a return to a more local economy. Everybody still lives in a parish, whether in town or country. It is best for the environment to grow and buy the food we need, and manufacture the goods we require, as locally as possible. 'Nothing is real unless it is local' (GK Chesterton). It is through our own town or parish council that we can most readily order local affairs.

Think about the prickles. Matthew takes a third of his gospel to recount the Passion of Jesus, who patiently suffered pain and humiliation and ultimately death. One of the symbols of his Passion is his crown of thorns pressed on to his head and the blood that stained his body.

Corn Cockle
Agrostemma githago

C orn cockles, cornflowers and corn marigolds number among several pretty cornfield flowers that have been almost exterminated by selective herbicides. Jesus told a story about tares and corn. The tares were probably darnel, a kind of grass that looks just the same as wheat until it is fully grown. By that time you cannot pull it up without pulling up the wheat as well. Furthermore it sometimes develops an associated fungus, which is poisonous. Only when the corn is harvested can you separate the one from the other. Jesus said, 'Let both grow together until the harvest' (Matt. 13.30). He used this to illustrate the truth that it is impossible to live this life in separation from all around us, and that judgement will come in the end, but only God can judge. Interestingly, it is a principle of organic farming and gardening to let crops grow without the intervention of pesticides and herbicides.

There is a special joy about gathering in the harvest, and seeing the results of work of every kind. In Vincent van Gogh's paintings golden corn is a symbol of resurrection. It is an ancient and vital custom to celebrate the harvest, and a harvest loaf is often specially baked for the festival. 'Give us our daily bread' is at the heart of the Lord's Prayer. It expresses our reliance on God for food and life, and our dependence on one another. Jesus said: 'Don't worry about tomorrow: tomorrow can look after itself' (Matt. 6.34). He also said: 'I am the bread of life' (John 6.35). He uses bread to convey himself in communion, at which bread is broken as a symbol not only of his death, but also of our duty to share. 'Whoever has a surplus has stolen it from his brother' (St Francis).

The book of Ruth is one of the great love stories of the world. Although Ruth was a foreigner, she insisted on accompanying her mother-in-law Naomi back to Bethlehem. Farmers were expected to leave some corn for poorer people to glean – a way of sharing their surplus. Ruth went gleaning in a field owned by Boaz, whom in due course she married. Their son was named Jesse, and David was their grandson, and so an ancestor of Jesus. The story is one of gracious and exemplary hospitality to a foreigner.

CORN
FLOWER

CORN
COCHLE

CORN
MARIGOLD

97

Great Bindweed
Calystegia sepium

Devil's guts is one of the many names of this convolvulus, indicating the gardener's frustration with such a troublesome weed, whose roots are very difficult to eradicate. Nevertheless the bell-shaped flowers of the bindweeds are very attractive as they twine round their neighbours in the hedgerows. More than most plants, their extensive root and branch systems provide a network dedicated to producing flowers and seeds to the best advantage. Good organization is vital for every corporate body, including churches. Jesus said: 'I am the vine: you are the branches' (John 15.5). St Paul identified administration as an important service to the early Christian Church.

A church has many different members – young and old, single and married, goodfits and misfits, Catholics and Evangelicals, charismatics and traditionalists, clergy and laity. St Paul told the Ephesians that, 'the whole body must be fitly framed together' (Eph. 2.21). The organization of the plant kingdom, which botanists have classified in orders, tribes, families, genuses and species, provides an interesting parallel. Subsidiarity is an important principle, first identified by the Franciscan, St Durandus of Pourcain, who said: 'there is no point in the greater doing what the lesser can do.' Delegation is vital in ministry as in all walks of life, as is accountability and proper support systems. The parochial system is the fundamental and vital building block in the Church of England. Everybody has a right to belong and a part to play.

Jacob's ladder is a lovely member of the Phlox family – distant cousins of the bindweeds. Its pinnate leaves look like little ladders. Jacob was on a long trek to escape from the anger of his brother Esau. He had tricked Esau out of his birthright, although it was his mother who had put him up to it. He was on the run not only from Esau, but also from God and from himself. He lay down to sleep beside a rocky precipice with a stone for a pillow. In his dream the precipice turned into a ladder with angels climbing down to care for him. In the morning he consecrated the stone with oil and called the place Bethel, which means God's house. We can be sure heaven is well organized. Good simple administration is so much better than convoluted (a word related to convolvulus) bureaucracy.

Spear Thistle

Cirsium vulgare

The names of thistles and their relations, like so many wild flowers, reflect the humour of our rural ancestors. The seed heads of thistles reminded them of shaving-brushes, although you would hardly shave with such a prickly implement! The closely related teasels were barber's brushes, too, but also church brooms, which prompts us to be grateful to all who clean our homes and churches, streets and public places. Teasels are still used for raising the nap of newly woven cloth. To tease comes to mean getting a rise out of people, and so leads us to one of God's precious gifts to humankind – the gift of laughter. Teasel's generic name is *Dipsacus*, which means thirsty, because water collects in the cups formed between leaves and stem. This water was once thought to have special healing properties. Laughter is a great healer.

There's more humour in the Bible than those who enclose it in black covers realize, such as Noah getting drunk, and Abraham's wife Sarah having a baby at a great age and calling him Isaac, which means laughter. The Proverbs include some sly fun: 'Go to the ant thou sluggard, and learn of him' (Prov. 6.6). Many of the stories of Jesus were surely told with a twinkle, like the host going out and collecting up all the down-and-outs to enjoy his dinner party when the invited guests didn't turn up. The 16th-century Italian saint, Philip Neri, was a renowned comedian. Another great wit wrote this verse about him:

Two books he read with great affection – the gospels and a joke collection,
And sang hosannas set to fiddles, and fed the sick on soup and riddles.
So when the serious rebuke the merry, let them remember St Philip Neri,
1515 to 1595, who was the merriest man alive:
Then dying at 80 or a bit, was made a saint by holy wit. (Ronald Knox)

The scabiouses are related to thistles. One of them is called devil's-bit scabious, because the root looks as if someone has taken a bite out of it, but the devil couldn't stop it producing its purple flowers. These little tight-packed heads are sometimes called bachelor's buttons – a name that was given to many small flowers, because fancy buttons were once a way of attracting a mate.

100

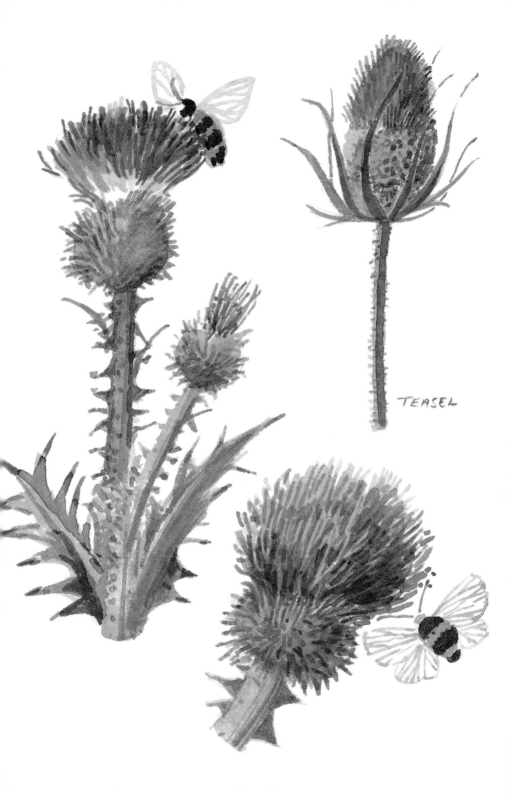

TEASEL

Water Mint

Mentha aquatica

A rich scent of peppermint arises when you tread on water mint found in damp places. Mint is one of many herbs that greatly enhance our lives. King Ahab coveted Naboth's vineyard because he wanted it for a herb garden. Most herbs are unspectacular, but growing in patches or in a formal knot-garden, they make beautiful patterns as well as being useful. Jesus ridiculed the Pharisees for being so fastidious as to tax mint. Mint would have been one of the bitter herbs served with lamb at the Passover supper. Herbs are symbols of voluntary service, which is often unspectacular and unrecognized, but it is all the stronger in liaison with others in a network of care. The voluntary sector remains a vital part of the national economy.

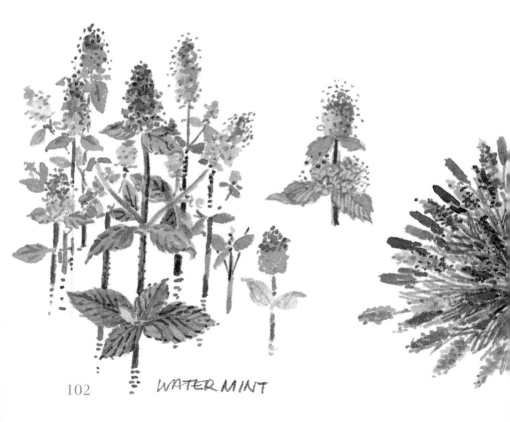

WATER MINT

The servant should always respect the patient, pupil, citizen, customer or client as a fellow human being. It is a madness of modern life that while so many care personally for others, vast organizations no longer regard people as people but nuisances at the other end of the phone. Service has been turned into a marketable commodity instead of a human kindness.

Mint has lots of herbal relations. Insects especially love wild marjoram. Its garden relation, pot marjoram or oregano, together with thyme, another cousin, are important ingredients of what the French call *herbes fines*. The mint family also includes basil, which is so good with tomatoes and is an essential ingredient of pesto sauce; another member is sage for stuffing. Although lavender is not a native plant, it is widely cultivated and a favourite ingredient. Its exquisite perfume in soaps, scents and fresheners is a great delight. The women who embalmed the body of Jesus could well have used lavender, which grows so freely around the Mediterranean.

So mint and its relations are symbols of service but also reminders of Jesus who said: 'I no longer call you servants but friends' (John 15.15), after he had washed the feet of his disciples and Peter had tried to stop him. That was during the supper at which Jesus was the waiter as well as the master of ceremonies – the servant of the servants, who were also his friends.

LAVENDER

MARJORAM

Reed

Phragmites australis

Reeds are graceful grasses, lovingly painted by Sir Peter Scott in his waterscapes. When Jesus spoke to the crowds about John the Baptist, he asked them: 'What did you go out to see – a reed shaken by the wind?' (Matt.11.3) The grass family is of enormous benefit to humanity and reeds are still used for thatching. Most cereals are grasses. They provide food for countless creatures including domestic animals, which transform it into milk and meat. Bamboo and sugar cane, pineapples and ginger, cardamom and turmeric, arrowroot and bananas are all exotic members of the same tribe of plants.

The papyrus sedge is justly famed. Moses' mother wove its leaves into a basket to save her baby son. The Egyptians manufactured paper from papyrus. The inner bark was called biblos, and indeed was the material on which the documents that comprise the Bible were first written. The Bible is a veritable library of myth, history, law, poetry, biography, letters and dreams. To interpret it requires ascertaining its original context, penetrating to its kernel through many layers of editing, understanding myth and parable, and relating its message to present circumstances. St Paul wrote to young Timothy that, 'all scripture is profitable for teaching, for reproof, for correction and for training' (2 Tim. 3.16). Scholars have uncovered immense riches in their researches, and translators have made God's word intelligible to millions. Notable among them are William Tyndale, and King James' team of translators who produced the first authorized version. Reading is a skill to be learnt – what to skim, what to study phrase by phrase, what to mark and what to inwardly digest. Many find it helpful to study the Bible in company.

Although paper is now usually a renewable resource, its production consumes energy and contributes to global warming. The western world consumes far too much paper. It is a good discipline to refuse unnecessary packaging, limit letters and circulars to one sheet, recycle all used paper, and only buy recycled paper.

Mushroom
Fungi species

M ushrooms and toadstools are plants without
chlorophyll, drawing their sustenance
mostly from dead materials. Many
of the thousands of species are edible, like the
famous truffle, but many are poisonous such
as the beautiful fly agaric. Yeast is a fungus
– which Jesus called the 'leaven in the lump',
and used it to illustrate the secret working of
the kingdom of heaven. Penicillin is another
fungus of great blessing.

Mosses, liverworts and horsetails, the oldest
species of living plants, are also distantly
related to fungi. Lichens are combinations
of algae and fungi. A species of lichen was
a source of blue dye in biblical times.
Lichens are litmuses of atmospheric
quality, being very vulnerable to
polluted air. Many rare species
grow only on churchyard
tombstones. They are often
centuries old and of great beauty,
and should not be scraped off.
These ancient plants recall
the fascination of history,
and importance of knowing
something of our origins.
'He who does not remember
history is bound to relive it'
(George Santayana). To
keep in mind a simple
historical framework
helps to keep life in
perspective.

106

The universe came into being perhaps 15 billion years ago, and the earth some 5 billion. It is about 300 million years since life first emerged on planet earth, 200 million years since animals began to move, and 2.5 million years since man stood on his own two feet. Roughly 4,000 years ago Abraham set off on his epic journey. About 3,300 years ago Moses led the people through the wilderness. About 3,000 years ago King David ruled Israel. Some 2,500 years ago the Buddha received his enlightenment. To remember one's ancestry is good for the soul and a filial duty for thoughtful people.

To live happily requires a balance between past, present and future. Although the present moment is all-important, it is necessary to keep one eye on the past and the other on the future. We need historians and recorders as well as prophets and visionaries, brakes as well as accelerators. Many mushrooms and their relations thrive on dead materials. They transform the past into present use. In their paintings the Chinese sometimes include the beautiful orange fungus *Ganoderma lucidum*, as a symbol of eternity. This fungus also grows wild in Britain.

Poppy

Papaver rhoeas

The gall the soldiers offered Jesus to drink on the cross, and which he refused, was the juice of the opium poppy, a close relation of the poppies that sprang up in their millions on the fields of Flanders (a typical poppy plant produces some 1,700 seeds). The poppies and the memorials are beautiful and so is the supreme sacrifice of those who lay down their life for others – the most loving and noble act that any human being can do. But let not the beauty disguise the ugliness. Those who have fought in wars are often reticent to describe their experiences, but the world needs to know the horror of it all. Poppies are red and black and green. The red reminds us of the carnage of war. They sprang up where the earth had been blighted and ravaged, and where the blood of millions had been spilt. The centres of the poppies are black. What is the cause of war? It is simply the sins of greed and envy – of taking privileges and profits, which have neither been given nor deserved, or sometimes even needed.

Jesus did not say: 'Blessed are the pacifists', but 'Blessed be the peacemakers'. There are in Christian tradition three main justifiable conditions for resorting to force. The first is to defend justice or prevent injustice – never for aggrandisement. The second is that it be carried out with the least possible violence or constraint, and without resort to torture, abuse or wholesale destruction. The third is that it be under proper authority or a last resort, and never out of personal acrimony or pure revenge. But the main cause of an unjustified war, whether worldwide, local or personal, is not at all complex. It begins in the nursery when one child says to another, 'I want that,' and the other child says, 'No, you can't have it – it's mine.'

The poppies have green leaves as well as red flowers with black centres. Those green leaves revive the hope that new life may grow. Poppies can be used for evil purposes. Opium poppies produce opiate or gall – the drug Jesus refused on the cross – and heroin, which many think is a greater threat to civilization than war itself. But it is the seed of those same poppies that bakers sprinkle on bread, imparting to it a subtle flavour. Instead of greed and envy, we must cultivate peace and love. We must support all efforts to negotiate peaceful settlements and resist the manufacture and sale of armaments. We must recover neighbourhood and neighbourliness. We must let our minds and hearts be filled with the subtle flavour of Christ's presence. That is the best antidote to war.

Great Mullein

Verbascum thapsus

Mulleins are tall stately plants, which remind people of a staff, so it is sometimes called Aaron's rod, recalling his rod that was turned into a snake, and swallowed up the snakes of Pharaoh's magicians. Aaron used his rod as a wand to launch the plagues of Egypt. Eventually he planted it in the ground and it grew and blossomed into an almond tree. Mullein gets its name from its emollient or soft leaves, which give rise to another of its names – Moses' blanket. Mulleins, therefore, recall the great heroes of the Old Testament – Abraham the patriarch, Moses the lawgiver (Aaron's younger brother), and David the singing shepherd boy who defeated the giant Goliath and grew up to be a king, a great composer and an ancestor of Jesus.

The human race is indebted to the Jews for the Ten Commandments – the bedrock of good law and government. Their fundamental laws, as they were developed and applied to many of the aspects of a settled life, enshrined much wisdom and caring concern even for animals. They decreed that an ox must not be muzzled, nor a hen killed when sitting on her eggs. The success of Jews in every department of life is due in part to their integrity, brilliance and hard work, which in turn are derived from their faith. Jesus worshipped in the synagogue. He taught that no jot or tittle of the Jewish law, known as the torah, should be broken, but that it was fulfilled in his teaching, life, death and resurrection. No one with feeling can fail to be outraged at the persecution of the Jews, which reached its appalling nadir in the Holocaust. There is wry truth in the remark made by a Jew in Auschwitz prison about the Nazi jailers: 'They are the ones behind the barbed wire.' Christians must, with shame, acknowledge that a wrong interpretation of the part played by Jews in the Passion of Jesus has contributed to anti-Semitism.

The toadflaxes are cousins of the mulleins. Toadflax is a favourite and widespread wild flower with its brilliant yellow and orange flowers. Ivy-leaved toadflax, which creeps over walls, is sometimes called wandering jew. The Jews have settled in many countries and enriched the world with their laws and psalms (spiritual songs) as well as their great artistic flair, business acumen and humour.

Lords and Ladies

Arum maculatum

Lords and ladies is an unusual wild arum. It has attracted many strange names including parson-in-the-pulpit. Quakers manage without an ordained ministry, which is a reminder that the most important priesthood is that of all believers. The only justification for commissioning special ministers is to help all members to minister.

Another old name for the plant is parson-in-his-smock. A minister has a wardrobe of special clothes or vestments, not unlike the sepals and petals of a flower. They provide clues to the work of ministry. The cassock is really an overall like a monk's habit for everyday wear, especially prayer. It is easy to stand, sit or kneel in a cassock, and it is warm in winter and cool in summer. When leading worship, the priest may wear a surplice or alb. These garments are crisp and white for purity and for the truth, which the clergy must proclaim and live. Starch was once made from the roots of the wild arum. The hood is an academic robe, originally for going out and braving the weather and so a reminder that teaching must not be confined indoors. The scarf was originally part of the hood. The stole recalls the towel with which Jesus washed the feet of his disciples. It is a long cloth worn round the neck like a yoke, especially in the sacraments. The chasuble is a reminder of the seamless robe of Jesus for which the soldiers gambled with dice at the foot of the cross. It represents the eternal love of God, and our love for him, especially in Holy Communion, at which the priest is privileged to preside. A cope is really an overcoat for processions, and is often richly embroidered. Every minister must beware of pride of status, and remember that robes reflect Jesus transfigured with the glory of God.

The ordained ministry of most churches now rightly includes women as well as men. Ministers are often privileged like lords and ladies, but they are sometimes subject to over-expectation and so to the danger of stress. As in most people's lives, the strength to resist stress includes proper management of time, delegation, rest and recreation, and sometimes saying: 'No'. Appraisal, training and support are vital, as well as an occasional change of scene. Games can be good relaxation as well as training in organizational skills. Parson Woodforde used to play card games with his friends and sometimes noted in his diary that he was 'exceeding merry!'

Holly

Ilex aquifolium

I t is an old custom to put a sprig of holly on top of the Christmas pudding. Many of the ingredients of the pudding remind us that Bethlehem is in a Mediterranean country. The raisins, sultanas, currants and peel come from warmer lands than ours. To mix such fruits with the homely products of our own country is to realize that Jesus was born into his own country, and yet his birth is for the whole world. Sweet chestnuts are cousins of holly. As you enjoy them roasted from your fire, or fill your turkey with chestnut stuffing, remember they too grow best in other lands.

The carol says: 'The holly bears a blossom as white as the lily flower.' Sometimes people say Christmas is for the children. It is, as long as you remember that we are all children. Mary gave birth to Jesus in obedience to God. There is a sense in which the mother of Jesus is the mother of us all. Through her travail she enabled us by God's grace to be born again ourselves and become children of God.

The holly leaves and berries shine. St John said: 'The light shines in the darkness and the darkness has not overcome it' (John 1.5). A partridge in a pear tree, in another well-known carol, is rhyming slang for the Latin phrase *parturit in aperto*, which means she gave birth in the open, that is, out in the stable. Jesus was born into the world – not just for human beings even, but for all creation. Jesus nestled in the hay, which represents inanimate creation and the complexity of all the manifold relationships of humanity and the created order. By tradition, the ox and the ass were there in the stable with the holy family. The star shining over Bethlehem lights up the characters in the Nativity. The holy family prompts our prayers for human families everywhere; the innkeeper for service industries; the shepherds for people at work; the wise men for rulers and authorities; and finally the ox and ass and hay for the rest of creation.

The holly is evergreen. Christmas opens for us the possibility of eternal life. This little baby Jesus is destined to suffer. The carol continues: 'The holly bears a berry as red as any blood and Mary bore sweet Jesus Christ to do poor sinners good.' We know that it is so often only death, especially the death of an innocent victim, which brings us face to face with the stark reality of pain and evil. Jesus will grow up to wear a crown of thorns and die on the tree of the cross to save the world.

Mistletoe

Viscum album

The ghostly white berries of mistletoe are associated with spells and witches. But this strange plant has good vibes as well. Some scholars say that the burning bush Moses saw was covered with a species of red-berried mistletoe that glowed like fire in the sunlight. Mistletoes are semi-parasites: they live partly off the host on which they grow. So there's something rather strange, even comical, about mistletoe. The saints have a great sense of humour and laugh at themselves and at the world. They smile with God who makes monkeys and frogs and giraffes. One of the great Christmas prophesies is Isaiah's charming vision of a peace that extends to the whole of creation. It surely contains a vein of humour. Wolves and sheep will lie down together. So will leopards and kids. Calves and lions will be friends, and lions will eat straw like cows, and children play over cobra's holes. There's time to play in heaven.

Mistletoe stays alive and green in winter and some lively fun in wintry weather keeps us young. The fun of pantomime relies on surprises. The dame is a man, and the prince is a girl. St Paul describes Christmas in this way: 'God purposely chose what the world considers nonsense in order to shame thee wise, and he chose what was weak in order to shame the powerful' (1 Cor. 1.27). The fact that God chose Mary to be the mother of Jesus is a great and beautiful mystery. But it is also profoundly astonishing, even humorous, that a carpenter's fiancée should give birth to the Son of God in a stable in the presence of an ox and an ass.

But the humour is really that of God himself as he springs his great surprise. His Son is born in a stable to an unmarried mother. Most people associate mistletoe with love, perhaps because its leaves always grow in pairs. The greatest love of all is the love of God who gives us this amazing present, the precious gift of his Son. This extraordinary act is a divine comedy if ever there was one.

Scots Pine

Pinus sylvestris

The pine is the nearest native relation of the fir. One Christmas Eve Martin Luther went out into the Black Forest in Germany to get some logs for the family fire. He had been wondering how best to teach his children that the light had come into the world. It was a dark night but the stars twinkled through the branches of the firs. He cut down a tree and took it home and fixed lighted candles to the branches. One can imagine the faces of his children when they saw the very first Christmas tree lit up in their home. Luther used the tree to teach his children about the light in the darkness. Darkness is a cover for plots and crimes and fantasies, but light reveals what is good and true and pure.

St John is celebrated on 27 December because the first chapter of his gospel is always read as a profound commentary on the birth of Jesus. John's symbol is an eagle because of his eagle-eyed insight into the mystery of Christ. John describes Jesus as, 'the Word or Wisdom of God made flesh' (John 1.1). His 17th chapter is the great prayer of Jesus for his disciples and for the world. Prayer is the means Jesus has given to us to remain his friends. 'Sum up at night what thou hast done by day, and in the morning what thou hast to do; dress and undress thy soul and mark the decay and growth of it' (George Herbert). Here is a simple extended form of the Lord's Prayer for busy people:

> *Our Father in heaven, hallowed be your name.*
> Study some scripture or contemplate an icon, and recite a creed (page 58).
>
> *Your kingdom come; your will be done, on earth as in heaven.*
> Recite the commandments (page 64), and confess your sins.
>
> *Give us our daily bread.*
> *Forgive us our sins, as we forgive those who sin against us.*

Give thanks and pray for:
The Church
Family, friends and neighbours
Education, work and leisure
The environment, justice and peace
Health and healing
The departed

Lead us not into temptation, but deliver us from evil,
for the kingdom, the power and the glory are yours,
now and forever.

About the Author and Illustrator

Anthony Foottit was brought up in a country vicarage and was the fifth generation of his family to be ordained. He was educated at Lancing, and King's College, Cambridge. Following his ordination, he served in team ministries in Norfolk and Somerset. His next appointment was as St Hugh's Missioner in his native Lincolnshire, before returning to Norfolk to become Archdeacon and then Suffragan Bishop of Lynn. He is now an assistant bishop and environmental officer in the diocese of Norwich. He is married to Rosie and they have three children. He has a lifelong interest in plants, especially wild flowers, gardening and conservation.

Pat Albeck was born in Hull, and studied Textile Design there, and then at The Royal College of Art. Since leaving The RCA, she has worked continuously designing fashion fabrics, furnishings, wallpapers, pottery and tins both in the UK and around the world. She has written and illustrated children's books, a text book for textile students, and *A Cat's Guide to England,* published in America, England and Japan. She has designed for museum shops and is especially known for her work for The National Trust shops. She has lived in Hull, London and, since 2000, in Norfolk. She is married to theatre designer Peter Rice. They have one son, designer, writer and painter Matthew Rice who is married to Emma Bridgewater, and four grandchildren.

Select Index
of Quotations

Bayley, John *Iris: A Memoir of Iris Murdoch* (Abacus 1999) 16
Bright, William *Hymns* (Publisher and date unknown) 39
Burke, Edmund *Selected Letters of Edmund Burke* (University Of Chicago Press 2000) 28
Donne, John *Meditation 17 No Man is an Island, from Devotions Upon Emergent Occasions* (Publisher unknown 1624) 82
Foster, Clare *Sharing God's Planet* (Church House Publishing 2004) 10
Herbert, George *The Church-Porch* (Publisher unknown 1663) 118
Knox, Ronald *Captive Flames: On Selected Saints and Christian Heroes* (Ignatius Press 2001) 100
Lehane, Brendan *The Power of Plants* (John Murray 1977) 8
Martin, W Keble *Over the Hills* (Michael Joseph 1968) 6
Pirsig, Robert *Zen & the Art of Motorcycle Maintenance* (Vintage 1991) 14
Sachs, Jonathan *The Dignity of Difference* (Publisher unknown 2002) 50
Santayana, George *The Life of Reason* (Promethus Books 1998) 106
Traherne, Thomas *Landscapes of Glory* (Darton, Longman & Todd Ltd 1989) 41
Waddell, Helen *Beasts and Saints* (Constable 1934) 92
Williams, Harry *True Resurrection* (Mitchell Beazley 1972) 42
Woodforde, James *Diary of a Country Parson 1758-1802* (Canterbury Press Norwich 1999) 113
Wordsworth, William *Intimations of Immortality* (Weidenfeld & Nicholson, 1995) 5
Young, Andrew *Collected Poems* Jonathan Cape, 1950 19

Acknowledgments

We thank Mic Cady and Ame Verso, our editors, for all their encouragement, and all who have inspired and helped us in the production of this book.